Plantations, Slavery &
FREEDOM
—— *on* ——
MARYLAND'S EASTERN SHORE

JACQUELINE SIMMONS HEDBERG

THE
History
PRESS

Published by The History Press
Charleston, SC
www.historypress.com

First published 2019

Manufactured in the United States

ISBN 9781467141024

Library of Congress Control Number: 2018958995

Notice: The information in this book is true and complete to the best of our knowledge. It is offered without guarantee on the part of the author or The History Press. The author and The History Press disclaim all liability in connection with the use of this book.

For Harry Boy, Patuson Tom and all the others

CONTENTS

CHARTS AND GRAPHS

PREFACE

When I retired from teaching many years ago, I thought that I had taught my last class. But, in the autumn of 2017, I found myself once again in the front of a classroom—this time teaching a course for Towson University's Osher Lifelong Learning Institute in Baltimore, Maryland.

That surprising turn of events happened because I read Edward Ball's article in *Smithsonian* magazine titled "Slavery's Trail of Tears."

I majored in U.S. history in college. And I know about the original Trail of Tears, when the federal government forcibly removed Indians from the Southeast to reservations beyond the Mississippi River. But before I read that *Smithsonian* article, I knew nothing about the million slaves who were forcibly relocated in the nineteenth century.

Why didn't I know *that* story? Why didn't I know about coffles—those trains of slaves, chained together, forced to walk more than one thousand miles from the Chesapeake to the slave markets of the South? Why didn't I know about Franklin & Armfield, one of the largest slave-trading companies in American history?

Some months after I read the *Smithsonian* article, my husband pointed out an item in the *New York Times* about 272 slaves who were sold in 1838 by the presidents of Georgetown College (what is today Georgetown University).

To sell such a large number of the college's assets at one time required approval from the Jesuit leadership in Rome. When those leaders worried about the loss of those souls, they were promised that the slaves would be able to continue to practice their Catholic faith, that families would not be separated and that the money raised from the sale would not be used to pay the college's debts. In the end, none of those three promises was kept.

Those 272 Georgetown slaves were a part of "Slavery's Trail of Tears." They were some of the million men, women and children from Maryland, Virginia and the rest of the Upper South who were moved to the cotton plantations and sugar cane fields of Alabama, Mississippi and Louisiana.

Those articles really bothered me because they described a migration that I knew nothing about. When I realized that many other people of my generation were ignorant of it as well, I set about preparing once again to teach.

I read probably one hundred or so books, journals and primary source documents in preparation for my class. Eventually, I decided that rather than solely dealing with the nineteenth-century internal slave trade, I would focus my lessons on an area of the country with which I have an intimate connection—Maryland's Eastern Shore.

I was born on Hoopers Island in southwestern Dorchester County, where my family has lived for more than 350 years. Some of my ancestors owned slaves. They treated slaves like property; used slaves as collateral for loans; freed some of their slaves; and, in at least one known case, had a slave run away. Some of my ancestors also sold land to a free black and became his next-door neighbors. That part of my past influenced both the content and the title of my class: "Free Blacks and Slaves on Maryland's Eastern Shore."

In our four classes, I talked about degradation and manumission, slave traders and abolitionists, overseers and free blacks. And I talked about "Slavery's Trail of Tears." We looked at why the relocation happened, who the big-name operators were and what routes were taken from Maryland and Virginia to the slave markets in Natchez and New Orleans. In our final lesson, we examined the Fugitive Slave Act, Harriet Tubman and the Underground Railroad.

Throughout these classes, we read records from the Maryland General Assembly, wills, deeds, inventories, bills of sale, memoirs and speeches. We examined maps and analyzed graphs and statistics. And, in each lesson, my students met people from my past—Henry Hooper, who owned plantations in both Calvert and Dorchester Counties; the second Henry Hooper, whose inventory at his death in 1720 included twelve slaves and a mulatto indentured servant worth £320; Hannah and Jhonah, who were equated with cows and furniture when Matthew Travers sold them to his son-in-law; Polly, who was used as collateral for Elizabeth Travers's $117 loan; Levin Parker, who freed Nell and her young sons Daniel, Jacob and Abram; and Thomas Bishop, who was not only freed but also given the right to vote.

After the final lesson, several people in my classes suggested that I publish this story about slavery on the Eastern Shore. The text which follows is the result.

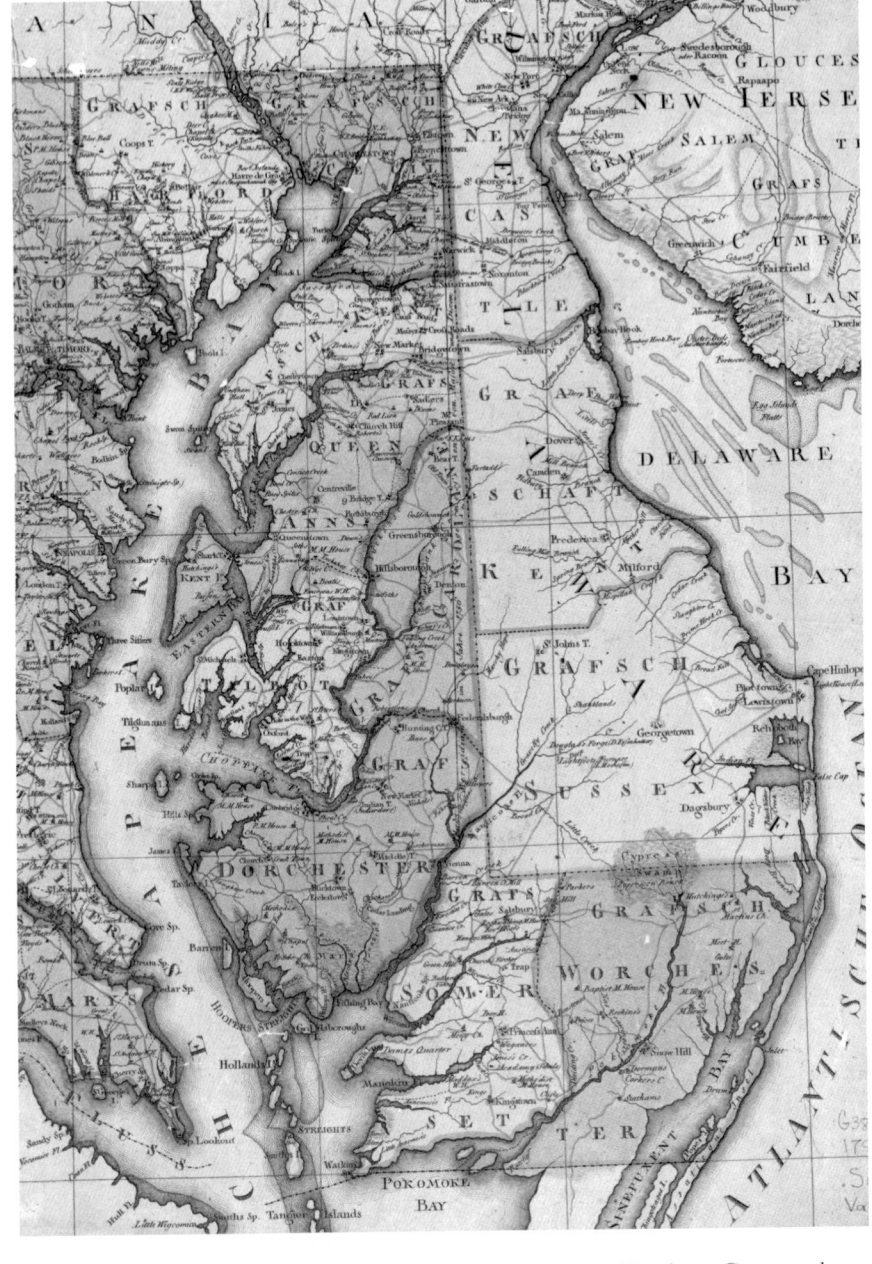

The Eastern Shore. Detail of *Maryland und Delaware*, published in Hamburg, Germany, by C.E. Bohn in 1797. *Courtesy of the Library of Congress, Geography and Map Division.*

COLONIAL MARYLAND TO 1750

Slavery is the condition whereby one human being has complete control of the life of another person. That relationship is based on power.[1] But slavery is not a static institution. Since the power on which it depends varies according to both time and place, there also is variance in the association between the master and the slave.[2]

Slavery on the Eastern Shore of Maryland existed from colonial times to 1864. It was a different institution in the first part of its settlement than it was one hundred years later at about the time of the American Revolution. Likewise, it was different in 1800 than it was sixty-one years later at the beginning of the Civil War. And slavery on Maryland's Eastern Shore was different from slavery in the counties of southern Maryland or slavery in the Deep South.

A FRAMEWORK FOR OUR ANALYSIS

The historian Ira Berlin divides communities that include individuals who are totally under another's power into two types. Some are what he calls "societies *with* slaves." Others he labels "slave societies."[3]

In "societies *with* slaves," slaves are marginal to the economic system; they are not the main labor force.[4] In the New England colonies, for example, the relatively few bondsmen in those colonies were not central to how most people there made a living, and slave owners in those colonies were just one portion of the propertied elite. The conditions under which slaves lived in such societies varied. Some owners treated their slaves with respect; other owners were cruel.[5] That said, slaves living in these societies were able to meet among themselves and move about relatively freely. They could grow crops, raise livestock and market their products. They could even save to buy their own freedom.[6]

In contrast, in "slave societies," slavery was essential to the economy, and slave owners were the ruling class.[7] Slaveholders in these societies monopolized economic resources. They pushed the small farmer to the periphery and consolidated their political power. (Many small farmers moved away.)[8] In these societies, most white people treated all their inferiors as if they were

Dorchester County, 1795. *Courtesy of Freepages.rootsweb.*

slaves. And the prerogatives that slaves once openly had were limited or abolished. Owners made it more difficult for slaves to obtain freedom, and they justified all their behavior as following some rule of nature or the law of God.[9] In the first century of its settlement, Maryland's Eastern Shore had both of these types of societies.

To put colonial Maryland into perspective, this first chapter examines in broad terms slavery in general, slavery on the North American mainland and the introduction of slavery into the Maryland colony. Consideration then is given to the impact that the tobacco economy had on the labor force, how slavery became institutionalized in Maryland and what forces combined to turn the colony into a "slave society." All of those things had an impact on how free blacks and slaves were treated in the counties on the eastern side of the Chesapeake Bay—from Cecil County in the north to Somerset and Worcester Counties in the south.[10]

Many of the examples in this chapter and those that follow will come from Dorchester County. Even more specifically, many references will be made to Hoopers Island, the community in the southwestern part of the county where my slave-owning ancestors lived. Land was first patented there in 1659, ten years before Dorchester County was established. It is the oldest settlement in the county. In the quoted material in these chapters, original spelling has been preserved.

WHERE SLAVERY ON THE EASTERN SHORE BEGAN

Slavery on the Eastern Shore of Maryland did not develop in a vacuum. In the Western Hemisphere, slavery came about as an extension of the Age of Exploration in Europe. First, the Portuguese (and then other Europeans) transformed small fishing villages along the western coast of Africa into trading centers.[11] In these villages, traders exchanged European textiles, metal products, guns, liquor and beads for African gold, ivory, hides, pepper and slaves.[12] Slaves, in these transactions, were merely one commodity among many. Europeans, most of all, wanted gold.[13]

By the time Europeans began to colonize mainland North America in the early seventeenth century, people of African descent could be found living all along the Atlantic coast of Europe, from Spain to England. Not all Africans living in Europe at this time were slaves, and not all slaves in Europe were of African descent. Slaves in Europe came from India,

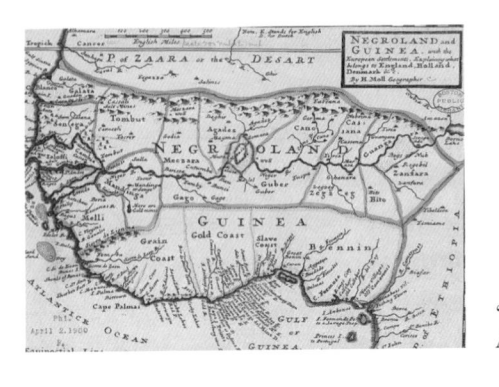

"Negroland and Guinea." Coast of West Africa, 1732. *Courtesy of Wikimedia Commons.*

China, the Crimea, the Caribbean, the Middle East and Eastern Europe as well as from Africa. The English had had slaves since the time of the Roman settlement there.[14]

One major African trading center was Port Saint George del Mina, located almost in the middle of the southern Gold Coast of Guinea. Del Mina means "of the mine"—as in gold mine. Eventually, the town came to be known simply as "Elmina."

As more European countries became involved in the African trade, the populations of coastal trading posts like Elmina ballooned. To give you some idea of just how much they grew, in 1664, when the English took over the Dutch North American trading post of New Amsterdam, that settlement had about 1,500 inhabitants. Elmina, at the same time, with its population of over 8,000, was more than five times the size of the Dutch settlement.[15]

Gold supplies in Africa dwindled in the 1600s. At the same time, sugar cane plantations were being developed on the Portuguese islands of the Azores and Madeira and, in the Western Hemisphere, in Brazil. The slave trade boomed as the demand for labor in the sugar cane fields grew.[16]

EARLY SLAVERY ON THE NORTH AMERICAN MAINLAND

In the Western Hemisphere, African slavery was introduced in 1501 in Santo Domingo, the first seat of Spanish government in the West Indies. Gold there, too, was the lure. After King Ferdinand received complaints that Indians could not do the work in the mines, he authorized sending two hundred Africans to work there.[17]

In 1526, the Spanish attempted to make a settlement on the North American mainland. They sent six hundred people (including slaves) and eighty to one hundred horses from Santo Domingo to what is today southern Georgia. The settlement failed—the leader died, and the slaves rebelled. The surviving Spanish went back to Santo Domingo, leaving the slaves to live or die with the Indians. How many survived is unknown. They are referred to as *cimarrones* or *marrons*. They are the first free blacks living on the North American mainland.[18]

In 1565, St. Augustine was settled in what would come to be northern Florida. After 1693, that settlement became a refuge for runaway slaves from the British colonies just to the north. The king of Spain—then at war with Britain—declared St. Augustine a safe haven if slaves converted to Catholicism.[19] Fort Mose, north of St. Augustine, became a military outpost—the first free community of ex-slaves in America.[20]

In 1607, almost half a century after St. Augustine was settled, Jamestown became the first permanent British settlement in North America. By 1619, Africans had arrived in the Virginia colony. According to a letter sent to London by John Rolfe, in late August 1619, a Dutch man-of-war landed "20. and odd Negars."[21] *Negar* is a Portuguese word meaning "black." Fifteen of these blacks went to work on Governor George Yeardley's plantation as indentured servants. The governor had exchanged foodstuffs for their contracts.[22]

In 1626, New Amsterdam was settled on Manhattan Island by the Dutch West India Company. During the first half of the seventeenth century, New Amsterdam had more slave labor than any other mainland colony. By the time Maryland was settled in 1634, close to one hundred slaves lived in New Amsterdam. They were roughly 10 percent of the port's population and a still larger percentage of the labor force.[23]

The slavery that evolved in the North American mainland colonies was different from that found in many other areas of the world. First, it connected slave status with people of color. (In Europe, even *blancos/* whites could be slaves.)[24] In the North American mainland colonies, children inherited their legal status (be it free, indentured or slave) not from their fathers, as had been the case in Europe, but from their mothers. And since the legal status of enslaved women was transferred to their offspring forever (freeing a woman did not free her children), slavery in North America was not just lifelong but hereditary.[25]

THE MARYLAND SETTLEMENT

Maryland was the personal estate of the Calvert family. King James I of England was a good friend of George Calvert, who for many years was clerk of the Privy Council. For his service to the Crown, Calvert was rewarded with a knighthood, a tract of land in Newfoundland, more than three thousand acres of land in Ireland and the title Baron of Baltimore.[26]

In 1632, King James's son King Charles I awarded George Calvert's eldest son, Cecil Calvert, a large tract of land located in an area then seen by the Virginia colonists as their territory.[27] The king's grant was for land between the Potomac and Delaware Rivers as far north as the fortieth parallel and as far west as the headwaters of the Potomac, excluding any area already inhabited.[28] Since Virginia colonists had already settled on the lower Eastern Shore, that land did not belong to Lord Baltimore.[29] The king named the new colony Terra Maria, Latin for "Maryland," in honor of his wife, Queen Henrietta Maria.

To encourage others to settle in Maryland, Lord Baltimore could deed them parcels of his land. These land grants were called "head rights," so many acres per head. Cecil Calvert offered a grant of one hundred acres for each settler who came to Maryland and an additional fifty acres for each member of his family and for each servant that he brought with him.[30]

This was a generous gift when one considers how difficult it was for an ordinary Englishman to obtain property at home. In the 1600s, most people in England were peasants without land, under the heel of a nobleman. If a family owned land, by the rule of primogeniture, only the first-born male stood to inherit it. The head right system was abolished in 1683. Thereafter, settlers had to buy their own land.[31]

Lord Baltimore gave his land in the Maryland colony "in perpetuity" with full rights to develop, lease, mortgage, bequeath or even sell the property.[32] To officially bind landowners to the proprietor and to spell out all the details of the arrangement, Lord Baltimore issued patents. These patents indicated the number of acres being granted, the location of the land, the amount of rent owed to the proprietor and the time the rent should be paid. Essentially, settlers became Lord Baltimore's long-term tenants, and they acknowledged his authority. In return for the land, settlers were charged an annual fee called a "quit-rent." The quit-rent system provided the proprietor with income to defray the costs of his colony.

In March 1634, the *Ark* and the *Dove* sailed into the Chesapeake Bay with Maryland's first settlers. The two boats carried 17 gentlemen (mostly

Queen Henrietta Maria with her husband, King Charles I, and their sons. Oil painting by Sir Anthony van Dyck. *Courtesy of the Library of Congress.*

younger sons of the Catholic gentry), more than 100 ordinary people (mostly Protestants who were familiar with farming) and 2 Jesuit priests with their 9 servants—130 to 140 settlers in all. Lord Baltimore's brother Leonard Calvert came to serve as the colony's first governor.[33]

As proprietor of this colony, Lord Baltimore answered only to the king.[34] Within his grant, he could raise an army, create towns, establish courts and enact laws. And, he could appoint a wide range of officials to enforce the law, handle judicial affairs and protect his interests.[35]

The governmental system established for the Maryland colony essentially copied the form of government that existed in England in the early seventeenth century. The first administrative area was named St. Mary's County. Within the county, it was the sheriff who was responsible for carrying out the orders of the governor and the colonial Assembly. Justices of the peace decided local cases, witnessed land sales, recorded debts and legitimized contracts.[36] Most counties of the Eastern Shore of Maryland continued to have this county form of government well into the twentieth century, with all of their laws, including those dealing with slavery, coming from Annapolis. There was no charter government or home rule.[37]

The Maryland area was not especially conducive to settlement. Mortality rates in the early years of the colony's existence were high for all segments of the population. In the tidewater, people's bodies had to physically adjust to an entirely new environment—different climate, unfamiliar foods and diseases like dysentery, malaria and typhoid. Then, there was the mosquito.[38] Henry Callister, who was an agent for the trading company Foster Cunliffe & Sons of Liverpool, wrote home in 1743 about conditions in his new home on the Eastern Shore:

> *The country being altogether wild and savage…and immense forest filled with vermin of various sorts and sizes….We are swarming with Musketoes, worms of every sort, spiders, snakes, hornets, wasps, sea nettles, ticks, gnats, thunder and lightening, excessive heat, excessive cold, irregularity in abundance.*[39]

Settlers described their acclimating ordeal as "seasoning." Those who did not die often suffered months of fevers and debilitating weakness.[40] Later, the word *seasoned* appears in advertisements for slaves being sold.[41] It usually meant that the slaves had come from the West Indies and not directly from Africa and that they were already acclimated to the Western Hemisphere's environment.[42] Consider this 1784 advertisement for the sale of slaves:

Thirty Seasoned Negroes
To Be Sold for Credit, at Private Sale

AMONGST *which is a Carpenter, none of whom are known to be dishonest.*

Also, *to be sold for Cash, a regular bred young Negroe Man—Cook, born in this Country, who served several Years under an exceeding good French Cook abroad, and his Wife a middle aged Washer-Woman, (both very honest) and their two Children.* Likewise, *a young Man a Carpenter. For Terms apply to the Printer.*[43]

This seller wanted to emphasize that these thirty slaves were *seasoned*, and he also pointed out that all of them were honest. That was not the usual eighteenth-century perception of blacks.

Free blacks and slaves were an early part of the Maryland colonial experience. The first free black in the colony was Mathias de Sousa, a mulatto who came to Maryland with the original settlers in 1634. He was an indentured servant attached to Father Andrew White.[44] In 1638, after completing his four-year contract, he became a free man. As a servant, de Sousa had learned to sail, and once he had completed his contract, he made his living as a sailor and trapper, revisiting the Eastern Shore Indians he first had met with Father White.

In 1638, the same year that Mathias de Sousa became free, Lord Baltimore requested that his agent buy cattle, sows, hens and "Ten Negroes" for use on his Maryland properties. There is no indication whether these ten were indentured or slaves.[45] In March 1638, the word *slave* first appears in Maryland's legislative records. The members of the Assembly were dealing with the issue of citizens' rights in the colony. They passed an act that "all the Inhabitants of this Province being Christians (Slaves excepted) Shall have and enjoy all such rights [and] liberties," as Englishmen had at home.[46]

In 1642, Governor Leonard Calvert asked the mariner John Skinner to acquire for him "fourteene negro men slaves, & three women slaves of betweene 16 and 26 yeare old, able & sound in body & limbs."[47] At this time, there were no laws in Maryland legalizing or regulating the practice of slavery. But slavery obviously already existed. Inventories of the period list servants by name with the terms they still had to serve. "Negroes" who were listed by name and had no terms were apparently slaves for life. Hence, we can conclude that de facto slavery preceded laws legalizing the practice in the Maryland colony.[48]

THE EASTERN SHORE

Clearing forests and making homes in the wilderness was backbreaking work. But little by little, the population of the Maryland colony grew. Settlement expanded first north of St. Mary's County. New administrative areas were created there—Anne Arundel County in 1650 and Calvert County in 1654.[49]

Planters who had plantations in eastern Calvert County on the Chesapeake Bay could see the Eastern Shore from their western shore properties. My eighth-great-grandfather Henry Hooper had a plantation on Calvert Cliffs just north of where the nuclear power plant is today.[50] From "Hoopers Cliffs," he could see land in what would become Dorchester County. But he could not claim that land.

Although Maryland had been founded in 1634, Lord Baltimore delayed settlement of the lower Eastern Shore for more than two decades so that he and his investors might profit from the fur trade.[51] Silk-lined beaver hats were an emblem of status for the nobility and the landed gentry in England, so there was a big market for pelts.[52] As long as the trade in beaver pelts was prospering, settlement in the lower Eastern Shore was forbidden.

In the mid-seventeenth century, one pound of beaver pelts was worth slightly over one hundred pounds of tobacco. The Calverts licensed private traders in return for payment of "a tenth in weight or value" of all the beaver that was traded. As a result, Lord Baltimore's profits were significant.[53]

In 1659, when the beaver population had been almost decimated, Lord Baltimore finally opened the lower Eastern Shore to settlement.[54] Once the region opened, the English population there grew rapidly. Like the colonists on the western shore, these early Eastern Shore settlers first claimed land along the main bodies of water—the Nanticoke, Choptank and Tred Avon Rivers. Settlers became interested in the interior only after all the waterfront had been claimed.[55]

Increased settlement meant new administrative units. Talbot County was established about 1661 and Somerset County in 1666.[56]

NATIVE AMERICANS

One cannot talk about the Eastern Shore in the seventeenth century without talking about the Native Americans who inhabited the area.

As an aside, it should be noted that the first known cargoes of slaves to cross the Atlantic actually sailed from west to east. They were the hundreds of Indians whom Columbus sent back to Spain.[57] When the Spanish arrived in the Caribbean, the islands were densely populated. By the 1550s (that is, within sixty years), the native population had been decimated. In the first half of the sixteenth century, approximately 2,500 Indians were sent to Europe as slaves.[58]

In Maryland, Indians were not enslaved. Governor Leonard Calvert, who headed the original expedition to the colony, exchanged a collection of axes, hoes, cloth and hatchets with the Yaocomacoe Indians for land in what became St. Mary's County.[59] But the Indians living on the Eastern Shore were different from the Yaocomacoes. These Indians were migratory. Rather than living in permanent villages, they moved from one seasonal camp to another to gather food. They were primarily Susquehannocks in the north and Choptanks and Nanticokes farther south on the peninsula.[60]

Before Lord Baltimore opened the Lower Shore for settlement, he signed treaties with these Indians. The 1652 treaty with the Susquehannocks ceded to Lord Baltimore all the land between the Elk and the Choptank Rivers—essentially, all the northern Eastern Shore.[61] The 1659 agreement with the Choptanks, however, did not cede land. Rather, the Choptanks agreed that there would be peaceful relations and perpetual friendship between the Indians and the English. They consented to allow the English to settle their families and cattle "upon any land on the Easterne shoare belonging to the foresaid Indians without molestation or Trouble."[62]

Of course, the Indian leaders who signed this treaty did not realize that the English view of landownership was entirely different from their own. While Native Americans generally viewed the land as being held in common, colonists saw deeds and titles as giving them exclusive property rights.[63] As more English settlers came to the Eastern Shore, the Indians lost more and more of the land that they customarily used for hunting and

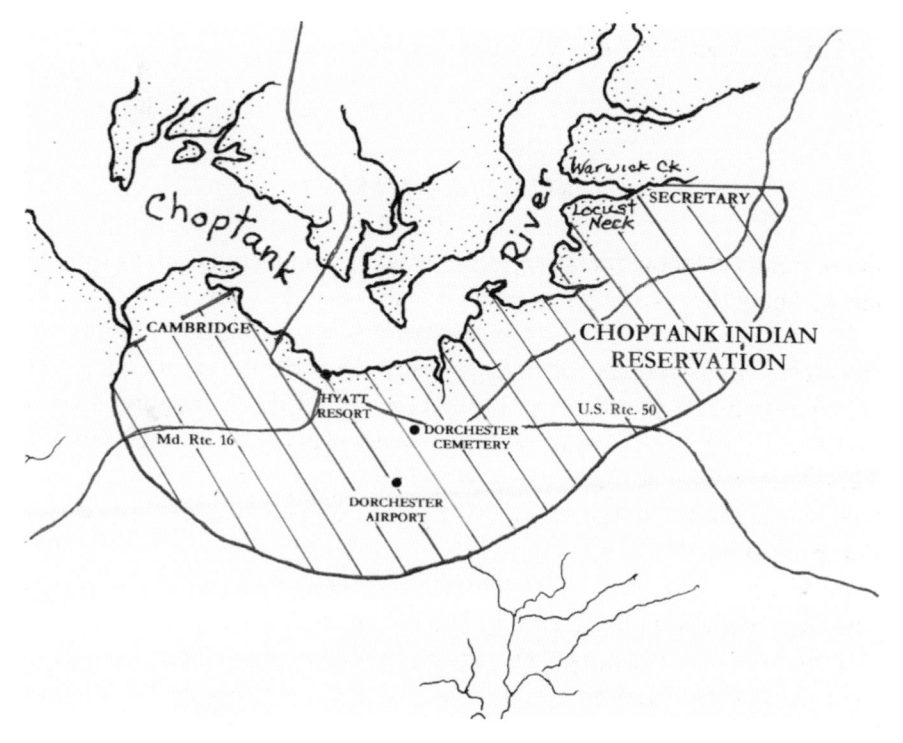

Modern roads imposed on a map of the Choptank Indian Reservation. *Courtesy of the author.*

gathering. When they finally realized that the English did not acknowledge any land rights except those granted by Lord Baltimore, the Indians asked the proprietor to legally guarantee them certain tracts of land.

In 1669, a grant was made to the Choptank Indians, and one was made to the Nanticokes in 1704, thus creating reservations on the lower Eastern Shore for these two Indian tribes.[64] The reservation lands given to the Choptank Indians were on the south side of the Choptank River. Their tract contained about nineteen thousand acres of land.[65] Today, when you drive Route 50 to Ocean City, you drive through the middle of the old reservation.

Discrimination against Indians at this time in Maryland was less than discrimination against blacks. There was no legal bar to assimilation. If an Indian male married a white woman, his children were considered white.[66] By the nineteenth century, however, all Indians in Maryland were classified as "free colored."[67]

THE TOBACCO ECONOMY

By the time Maryland was founded (and certainly by the time the lower Eastern Shore was opened to settlement in 1659), Virginia had already established tobacco as the money crop for the Chesapeake region.[68] The climate and soil of the region were suitable for growing tobacco, and the Chesapeake had so many navigable rivers that each plantation could send tobacco to market directly from its own wharf.[69] And the settlers had a strong European market for their product.

By the end of the seventeenth century, tobacco production in the two Chesapeake Bay colonies exceeded twenty million pounds a year. In 1775 (on the eve of the American Revolution), it exceeded one hundred million pounds. In that year, it represented 75 percent of the total value of all tidewater exports and was worth about $4 million.[70]

In a letter to Lord Baltimore in 1729, Governor Benedict Leonard Calvert summarized the role of tobacco in Maryland and pointed out the difficulties involved in growing the crop. He wrote:

> *Tobacco, as our Staple, is our all, and Indeed leaves no room for anything Else; It requires the Attendance of all our hands, and Exacts their utmost labour the whole year round. It is the most uncertain Commodity that Comes to Markett.*[71]

Maryland tobacco farm. *Courtesy of the Library of Congress.*

Colonial farmers in Maryland did not clear large fields of timber and then plow the soil. If they had, it would have taken them a month to clear an acre of forest.[72] Instead, they cut deep girdles through the bark around the tree trunks. This prevented the sap from rising, which, in turn, killed the trees. When the trees' foliage died, seedlings (planted in mounds of soil between the trees) had enough sunlight to grow. Since the colonists had few oxen or other draft animals to pull out the dead stumps, they were simply left in the fields, just as Benjamin Latrobe depicted in the 1798 watercolor sketch on the next page.

Tobacco seeds are planted in early spring in specially prepared beds. The seeds themselves are so small that one author remarked that "ten thousand may be accommodated in a teaspoon."[73] Once the seeds were planted, the seedbed had to be covered to protect against frost, watered when it was

An Overseer Doing His Duty, watercolor sketch by Benjamin Henry Latrobe. *Courtesy of the Maryland Historical Society, 1960.108.1.2.21.*

dry, thinned and weeded. While the seedlings were growing, farmers used hilling hoes to shape mounds of earth between the dead trees so that tobacco roots would be able to develop once the crop was planted. (That is what the slave women are doing in Latrobe's painting.) Then, in late spring when wet weather made the ground soft, the new seedlings were transplanted into holes in these mounds.[74]

About six weeks after transplanting, the stalks were topped to prevent flowering and ensure that large leaves would grow.[75] During the summer, the plants were continually weeded and suckers were cut off. They were also debugged. (Hornworms could devour a whole crop in just a few days.)[76] In late summer, when the leaves had turned to a yellowish-green, the mature tobacco plants were cut by hand and the leaves hung in special curing barns to dry. The strongly flavored Oronoco tobacco, which was grown by the planters on the Eastern Shore, usually took five or six weeks to cure.[77]

After the crop was properly cured, the stalks were taken down, bulked in piles and then layered into hogsheads. Each hogshead was marked with the owner's initials. The large barrels then could be rolled to the wharf and loaded onto boats that would transport the tobacco to England for sale.[78]

After 1747, all Maryland tobacco had to be shipped to the nearest inspection warehouse. There it was inspected for quality, re-barreled and then shipped to London. There were seven inspection stations in Dorchester County alone, including one in Hoopers Island—obviously, lots of tobacco was being grown on the Eastern Shore.[79]

All of this information about tobacco is meant to impress upon you two things: first, that planters in tidewater Maryland relied upon a crop that required large amounts of labor and second, that those laborers had to work, as the governor said, almost continuously "the whole year round."

What about the labor force? Who were the people growing the tobacco? Remember, first of all, that population in the entire Maryland colony was low. When the lower Eastern Shore was opened in 1659, the whole colony had a population of only about four thousand. (Look at the year 1660 on the graph below, "Estimated Population of Maryland.")[80]

The Eastern Shore of Maryland was sparsely settled. About 80 percent of the farmers there in the seventeenth century owned fairly small amounts of acreage. On these small farms, the planters, with the other members of their families, were their own total labor force. The remaining 20 percent of the farmers on the Eastern Shore, those who had some resources to hire others to help them, either purchased the contracts of indentured servants or bought slaves.[81]

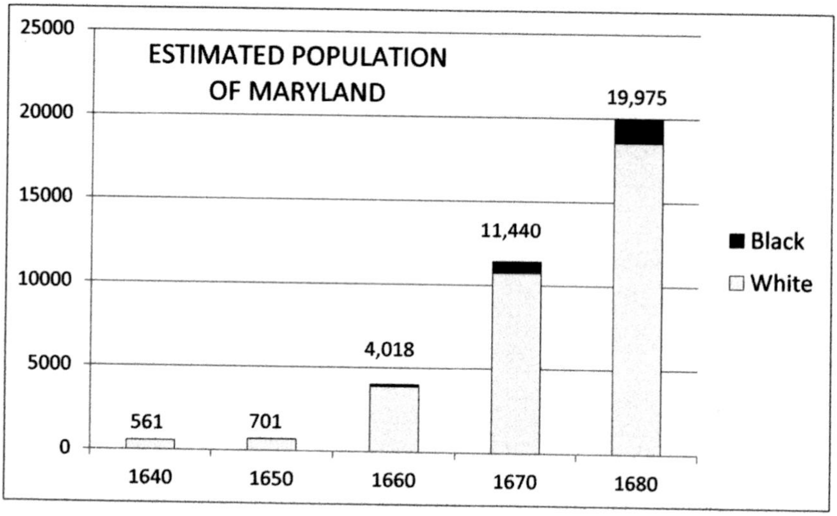

Graph 1. Estimated Population of Maryland, 1640–1680.

Most labor in the early colonial period was done by indentured servants with a set time to serve in exchange for their passage to the colony.[82] Many early settlers brought these servants with them, claiming land for each servant that they imported. When Henry Hooper came to Maryland in 1651, he brought three indentured servants and claimed fifty acres of land for each of them under the head right system.[83] Sea captains also transported servants, convicts and poor farmers and sold their contracts to colonial planters, who then could claim head rights.[84] Tobacco ships brought servants to America and then filled their holds with tobacco for the return trip to England. Two-thirds of all the first immigrants to the colonies south of New York were indentured servants.[85]

The earliest traders in slaves to Maryland were the Dutch.[86] Later, colonial seamen (especially those from New England) sailed to Barbados and other parts of the West Indies and brought seasoned slaves back to Maryland as part of their cargo. From 1663 to 1698, the Royal African Company had a monopoly on the slave trade to England's American colonies. During that period, the number of slaves brought to the Chesapeake Bay area was small—a few thousand in three decades.[87]

All the workers growing tobacco in this period (indentured servants and slaves) worked according to common English labor practices.[88] A work week was about five and one-half days in summer, with winter work reduced. Workers had Sundays, half-day Saturdays and holidays for themselves.[89] Masters provided their workers with sufficient food, clothing and shelter. Thus, in the middle years of the seventeenth century, slaves on the Eastern Shore had the same benefits that were extended to indentured servants.[90]

In this period, when they wished to discipline their workers (whether indentured or slave), colonists used the courts. (Not until the next century did planters presume that they were absolute rulers on their estates.)[91] Servants and slaves also sued in the local courts and petitioned the Assembly.[92]

ANTONIO, A NEGRO

In the first decades of colonization, *slave* and *Negro* were not synonymous. The story of one African can help to illustrate those times. While his story begins in Virginia, his family eventually became free blacks on Maryland's Eastern Shore.

"Antonio, a Negro"[93] worked on the Richard Bennett plantation near the James River in the 1620s. (It is not clear whether he was a slave or an indentured servant.) Antonio was loyal and hardworking, and the Bennetts appreciated those qualities. They allowed him to independently farm in his free time. Owners frequently allowed their workers to labor independently. Many gardened, tended barnyard animals and hunted and fished on their own, selling their catch. Sometimes they made small items and sold them. Some became skilled carpenters and shoemakers and sold their services.[94]

Antonio married, and his children were baptized. Eventually, Antonio became free. At that point, he took the name Anthony Johnson. In 1640, Anthony Johnson, his wife, Mary, and their four children followed the Bennetts to the eastern shore of Virginia. In this period, it was not uncommon for free blacks to cultivate and maintain relationships with their former owners.

In 1651, Johnson earned a 250-acre head right by buying the contracts of five indentured servants. The following year, however, he suffered great property loss by a devastating fire, and the family was given some tax relief by the Virginia courts. Anthony Johnson owned slaves. In 1653, when one of his slaves ran away, Johnson used the courts to get the slave returned.

About 1662, Anthony Johnson and his family migrated from Virginia to the Maryland colony, leasing a three-hundred-acre tract named "Tonies Vineyard" in Somerset County. The Johnsons might have been the first free blacks in the county.[95] The family stayed in Somerset County for generations. In 1677, there is a record of Anthony Johnson's grandson Francis Johnson buying a forty-four-acre farm there.[96]

The Johnsons held land, owned slaves, paid taxes, had access to the legal system, could borrow and lend money and could witness official documents. Thus, they were not much different from the white planters who were their neighbors.[97]

INSTITUTIONALIZING SLAVERY

Since many farms on the Eastern Shore were small, owners usually worked on their land side by side with both their indentured servants and their slaves.[98] And blacks and whites working shoulder to shoulder in the fields meant that racial lines were somewhat blurred. While the status of slaves was defined in practice, in this period, it remained undefined by law.[99]

It was the rather fluid racial boundaries in the colony that led to the first statute in Maryland institutionalizing slavery. In 1664, "An Act Concerning

Negroes and Other Slaves" was passed, defining slavery as being in servitude *Durante Vita* (for the duration of one's life), and it specified that all children born to slaves would themselves be slaves.[100]

The law's main purpose, however, does not seem to have been to define and regulate slavery. Rather, what the Assembly seemed to find objectionable was interracial marriage.[101] The legislators wanted to forbid freeborn English women from marrying black slaves. They described such unions as "shamefull Matches" and the "disgrace of our Nation."[102]

The 1664 law stipulated that upon such a marriage, the woman would serve the master of the slave that she had married for the rest of her husband's lifetime and all their children would be slaves.[103] (This part of the law was repealed in 1681 because some unscrupulous white masters were acquiring white female servants and then forcing these women to marry their slaves in order to enslave the women and their offspring.)[104]

This 1664 law not only institutionalized slavery, it was the first legal manifestation in Maryland of English disdain for Africans as well. European women who married blacks, the Maryland law said, were a disgrace to whites everywhere.[105] With this early law, we already begin to see the transmutation of the line between slave and free into a line between black and white.[106]

At this point in Maryland history, planters who could afford help were more likely to use English indentured servants rather than slaves. And when the General Assembly enacted legislation, it often considered servants and slaves together. We see that in a 1676 law, when it was enacted that no servants of whatever kind (indentured, slave or hired worker) could travel ten miles by either land or water without a note from their master, mistress, dame or overseer.[107]

It is important to note that blacks in seventeenth-century Maryland were still considered persons.[108] While their movement was somewhat restricted, they still could testify and sue in court; they were legal partners in contracts; and, in their "freedom petitions," they could present witnesses to speak on their behalf. (After 1664, some blacks still worked in Maryland under contract, with set terms of service.)[109]

In 1680, there were 1,611 slaves in the Maryland colony. Only 9 percent of the population was enslaved; Maryland's slave population was relatively small.[110]

When a person died in colonial Maryland, the local court appointed two people to inventory the deceased's possessions. All of those inventories can be read at the Maryland Archives in Annapolis. What historians have learned from researching those documents is that in 1680, indentured servants outnumbered slaves by almost four to one.[111] We can conclude from these inventory numbers that slaves were marginal to the Maryland economy in 1680; they were "just one form of labor among many."[112] The whole colony at that point, and certainly the Eastern Shore, could best be described simply as a society that included some slaves.

BECOMING A "SLAVE SOCIETY"

Then, at the end of the seventeenth century, a sweeping transformation took place in the Chesapeake. First, there was a rise in tobacco prices. And rising tobacco prices brought an increased demand for labor. At the same time, fewer Europeans were willing to come to Maryland as indentured servants. Wages were improving in England, and colonial Maryland had become less attractive for potential indentured laborers.[113] To a large extent, that was the consequence of an action taken by the General Assembly.

In its 1663 session, legislators repealed a clause in an earlier act requiring planters to make a gift of fifty acres of land to indentured servants when their terms of service were done. Instead, planters were required to give only "a servant's due"—a set of clothing (including shoes and a hat), a hilling hoe, a weeding hoe, a felling axe and three bushels of seed corn for planting.[114] That change was even more significant because rising land prices in Maryland made it very difficult for indentured servants to buy their own land when their terms of service were completed. Most of them, therefore, were forced into tenancy.[115]

Since there were fewer indentured servants coming to Maryland after 1663, planters began to rely upon slaves to fill the labor shortage.[116] More and more ship manifests specified cargoes of slaves to be delivered to Maryland.

The rising tobacco prices that enabled planters to purchase more slaves coincided with Parliament's abolition of the Royal African Company's monopoly on the slave trade in 1698.[117] Dozens of independent traders (many from New England) now joined the lucrative slave market to meet the increased demand. Generally, slaves coming to the Chesapeake came through the West Indies. They were just a small part of an immense international trade.

Slaves were more expensive than indentured servants. Economically, however, buying slaves made sense because slaves were valuable to their owners several times over. Once you bought a slave, you were entitled to that slave's labor for life. Slaves appreciated as they matured and learned skills. Children born to slaves automatically became slaves, so the slaveholder's labor force grew. And when owners sold their slaves, the sale usually made a profit.

In time, more and more large planters began using slaves as their primary labor source.[118] That change was revolutionary. During the last five years of the seventeenth century, more slaves were purchased by Chesapeake tobacco farmers than had been purchased in the previous twenty years.[119]

In April 1706, the legislature passed "An Act for advancement of trade and erecting Ports & Towns in the Province of Maryland." This law essentially created a number of official ports of entry for the colony.[120] The act stated that "the places mentioned shall be the Ports and Places where all Ships and Vessels trading into this Province shall unlade and put on shoare all Negroes Wares goods merchandizes and Comodities whatsoever."[121]

Notice that the act specified "Negroes," not "slaves" or "Africans" or "servants." The legislature was clearly separating people according to color.

When this trade act was passed, Maryland was still basically a tidewater colony. In 1710, almost half of its 42,741 population lived on the Eastern Shore.[122] There were twelve counties, six on each shore of the bay: Baltimore, Anne Arundel, Prince George's, Calvert, Charles and St. Mary's on the western shore and Cecil, Kent, Queen Anne's, Talbot, Dorchester and Somerset on the Eastern Shore.

The Chesapeake Bay and its tributaries were the highways of the colony. With almost equal populations on the two shores, the major traffic pattern was an east–west movement, and the water served as a bond to connect the widely separated plantations on both sides of the estuary.[123] In 1710, the colony's land boundaries were undefined, and Baltimore City did not exist.

While the map gives no hint of this, by 1710, the Maryland colony had begun to undergo tremendous change. That change was reflected in colonial inventories. Between 1698 and 1710, some six thousand slaves had been brought to Maryland, an average of five hundred per year.[124] Now, instead of indentured servants outnumbering slaves by four to one in the inventories (as we saw previously in 1680), the numbers had reversed. By 1710, there were roughly five slaves for each indentured servant, and more than 15 percent of the Maryland colony's inhabitants were slaves.[125]

This demographic change from servant to slave labor was clearly exhibited on the Eastern Shore. In 1680, the Shore's slave population was about 300. By 1704, it had grown to 1,390; by 1710, it was 1,640.[126] The change was readily apparent on Hoopers Island.

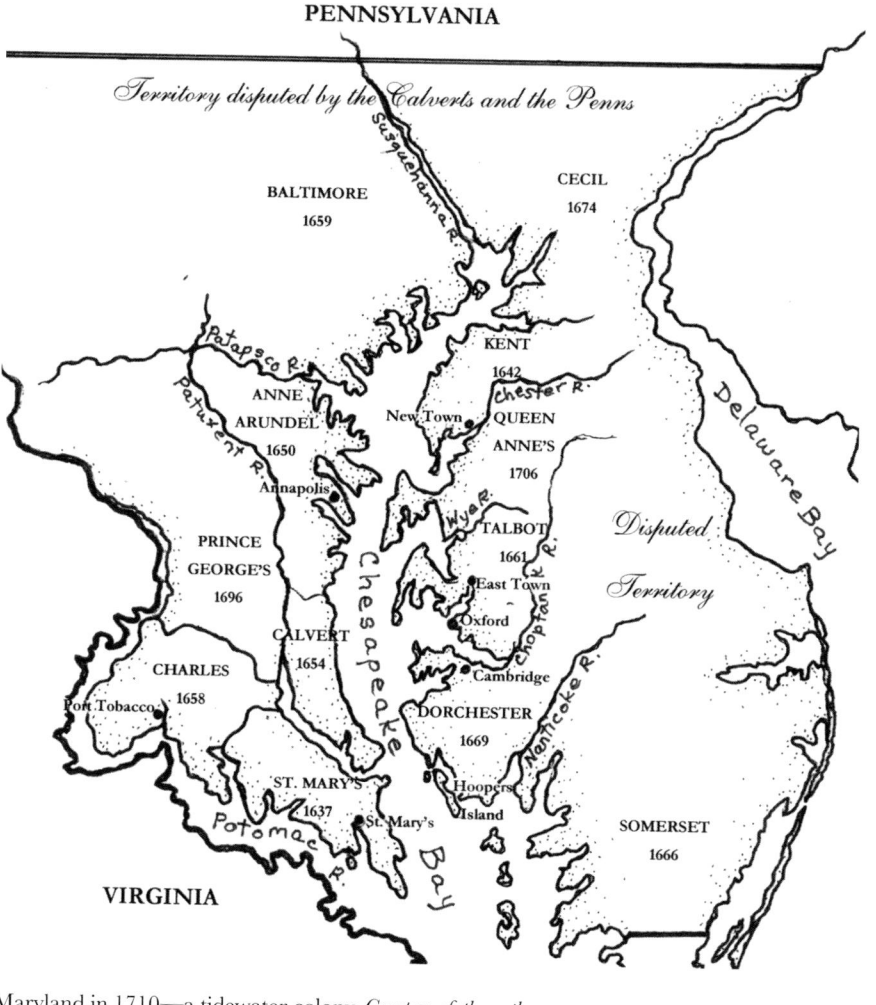

Maryland in 1710—a tidewater colony. *Courtesy of the author.*

Land on Hoopers Island was first patented by William Chapline, who used his three-hundred-acre property "Chaplin's Holme" to raise livestock. When he died in 1669, Chapline bequeathed his Dorchester County property to his daughter Elizabeth. She also inherited two servants who possibly were slaves.[127] Property adjacent to Chaplin's Holme was patented by the first Henry Hooper in 1668.[128] When he died, his son (also named Henry Hooper) inherited the property. The second Henry Hooper died in 1720.

WILLIAM CHAPLINE, 1669   HENRY HOOPER, 1720

One man-servant

One woman-servant

1 Negro man called Sambo

1 Negro man called Robin

1 Negro man called Tobias

1 Negro man called Frank

1 Negro man called Stephen

1 Negro woman called Nancy

1 Negro woman called Moll

1 Negro woman called Nan

1 Negro boy called Will

1 Negro boy called Harry

1 Negro girl called Pleasant

1 Negro girl called Sabine

A mulatto girl with 14 years to serve

£320

Chart 1. From Servant to Slave Labor on Hoopers Island.

In contrast to the two servants in William Chapline's estate, "Negroes" are the first items listed in Henry Hooper's inventory. He had twelve slaves and a mulatto girl who had fourteen years left to serve. Consider how valuable these slaves were. They were appraised at £320 sterling. Henry Hooper's inventory shows that he owned a considerable amount of livestock (cattle, horses, sheep and hogs). His livestock's value, however, was only £127.18.6—less than half the value of his human property.[129]

By the second decade of the eighteenth century, slightly over half the blacks coming to the Chesapeake came directly from Africa. And, by mid-century, the volume of imports from Africa reached 90 percent of the total.[130] The largest slave market in the British mainland colonies during the first decades of the eighteenth century was Charles Town, South Carolina. Slave sales were held right next to the wharves to make the sales convenient for local plantation owners, who could come by sloop from their riverside farms.[131]

On the Eastern Shore, there were importation points at New Town (Chestertown), East Town (Easton), St. Michaels, Oxford, Cambridge and Vienna. Some colonial merchants participated in the trade by receiving consignments of slaves from large British firms like Richard Gildart and Co. and Foster Cunliffe & Sons, both of which had resident agents in Oxford. (The locals knew which planters had good credit.) Robert Morris in Oxford was one of these agents. Morris received about 5 percent commission on his slave sales.[132]

By 1750, the Maryland colony as a whole was significantly different from what it had been in the seventeenth century. By then, Maryland had fourteen counties—seven on each side of the Chesapeake Bay. On the Eastern Shore, Worcester had been added in 1742. Population growth had led to an increase in the number of organized towns, including Easton, Chestertown, Salisbury and Cambridge. By the mid-eighteenth century, the population of Chestertown was second in size only to Annapolis.[133]

Baltimore Town (founded in 1729) was becoming a thriving port. By 1750, it was handling wheat exports from the Eastern Shore, western Maryland and the German farmers of Pennsylvania.[134] It also shipped pig iron that was being produced near the Patapsco River. And it had a vibrant shipbuilding industry.[135]

The *Maryland Gazette*, the first newspaper in the Chesapeake region, had been started in 1727 by William Parks of Annapolis.[136] Newspapers would become important for advertising offers for slave purchases, slave auctions and rewards for the apprehension of runaway slaves.[137] Some newspapers also promoted abolition.

The first regular mail route that included the eastern side of the Chesapeake had begun—once every two weeks in summer and once a month in winter.[138] And "An Act for the Encouragement of Learning…"

Masthead for an early edition of the *Maryland Gazette*, April 8, 1729.

had been passed in 1723 to erect a school in each county.[139] In 1745, a boarding school for boys in Chestertown advertised that it taught writing, arithmetic, merchants' accounts, surveying, navigation, the use of globes, several branches of mathematics, Latin, Greek, fencing and dancing. In many Eastern Shore counties, however, it was difficult to establish a school in a location that would be accessible for most of the population.[140]

And by 1750, something else had happened. Population statistics in the graph "Slave Population in Maryland" tell the tale.[141] Maryland had gone from 1,611 slaves in 1680 to 43,450 slaves in 1750. Slaves were now almost one-third of the colony's total population.[142] The change from 1720 to 1750 is quite dramatic. It is obvious that by 1750, slaves were no longer marginal in colonial Maryland. The state (including the Eastern Shore) had become a "slave society."

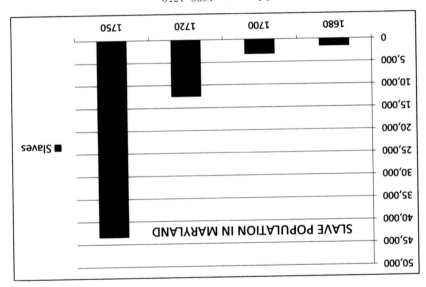

GRAPH 2. SLAVE POPULATION IN MARYLAND, 1680-1750.

IN SUMMARY

The history of slavery on Maryland's Eastern Shore during the first century of its settlement can roughly be divided into two parts. In the area's first fifty years—from about 1659 to 1700—the area was sparsely settled (mostly along the waterfronts). Most farms were small. Everyone grew tobacco (and, therefore, everyone worked year-round). Owners, indentured servants and slaves all worked in the fields together according to common English practices. And there were four times as many indentured servants as slaves.

In the colony's second fifty years—from about 1700 to 1750—slaves began replacing indentured servants on the Eastern Shore. (Fewer indentured servants were interested in coming to Maryland.) Most slaves came directly from Africa, not from the West Indies. And, by 1750, slaves had become essential to the economy. The Eastern Shore had become a slave society.

2

TWO REVOLUTIONS

By the middle of the eighteenth century, tobacco reigned in the Maryland colony, and almost one-third of the population was enslaved.[143] The Chesapeake had been transformed into a slave society—one that was dependent upon slave labor. That transformation is called the "Plantation Revolution."[144]

THE PLANTATION REVOLUTION

The word *plantation* often conjures up a romantic picture of a manor house surrounded by landscaped gardens. Maybe we even think of ladies in hoop skirts and mint juleps being served on a columned veranda. But there is another side to the plantation picture that is not quite so pretty—that of the slaves who made the plantation owner's life of leisure possible.

Both pictures—that of the manor house and the slave's shackles—accurately illustrate the Plantation Revolution on Maryland's Eastern Shore.

By 1750, tobacco had made slaves a central part of the Maryland economy, and large plantation owners had taken control of the colonial government. The slaveholders' seizure of power is the critical event that transformed society.[145] Only the wealthy had the capital to afford a large enslaved workforce.[146] Planters who controlled capital pushed small farmers from the countryside and monopolized the best land. Many small farmers from the Eastern Shore moved to the Piedmont or the Carolinas.[147]

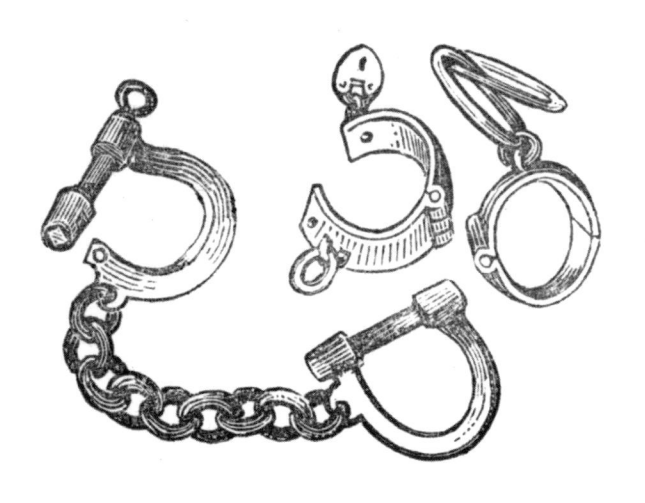

Shackles used
to restrict slaves.
*Courtesy of the Library
of Congress.*

Slave owners dominated eighteenth-century Maryland's colonial government. In 1750, in Annapolis, Edward Lloyd from Talbot County with his 176 slaves was in the Upper House and on the Governor's Council. In the Lower House, delegates who represented the Eastern Shore owned among themselves hundreds of slaves. These 8 members alone owned 66,515 acres of land and 461 slaves.[148] And the laws these men passed certainly reflected their own interests.[149]

By the early eighteenth century, the philosophy of the times had changed. Instead of saying that slaves deserved to be slaves because of their own behavior (they had lost in battle, they were criminals or they were debtors), slaves were now described as inferior in their use of reason or incapable of leading a life of reason.[150]

SELECTED MEMBERS OF THE MARYLAND LEGISLATURE IN 1750

- Edward Lloyd (Talbot)
- Robert Jenkins Henry (Somerset)
- Thomas Robins (Worcester)
- Robert King (Somerset)
- Nicholas Goldsborough (Talbot)
- John Goldsborough (Talbot)
- Henry Hooper (Dorchester)
- John Selby (Worcester)

CHART 2. SELECTED MEMBERS OF THE MARYLAND LEGISLATURE IN 1750.

Thomas Jefferson, in his *Notes on the State of Virginia*, reflected that idea when he wrote that "blacks, whether originally a distinct race, or made distinct by time and circumstances, are inferior to whites in the endowments both of body and mind."[151] The logic went that, since slaves were not intelligent enough to direct their own lives to reach fulfillment, they profited from having their lives directed by others.[152]

That condescending attitude persisted well into the twentieth century.[153] Samuel Eliot Morison and Henry Steele Commager authored the highly regarded textbook that I used in 1957 as a freshman at Western Maryland College. In it, they wrote:

> *As for Sambo…there is some reason to believe that he suffered less than any other class in the South from its "peculiar institution." The majority of slaves were adequately fed, well cared for, and apparently happy. Competent observers reported that they performed less labor than the hired man of the Northern states.…Although brought to America by force, the incurably optimistic Negro soon became attached to the country, and devoted to his "white folks."*[154]

And, the authors went on:

> *If we overlook the original sin of the slave trade, there was much to be said for slavery as a transition from a primitive to a more mature culture. The Negro learned his master's language, received his religion, and accepted his moral standards. In return he contributed much besides his labor—rhythm and humor for instance—to American civilization.*[155]

By the beginning of the nineteenth century, southerners had decided that slavery was a positive good. This theory was based on the ideas that slavery was necessary to economic development of the South, blacks were biologically inferior, slavery was a means of converting heathens to Christianity and slavery had enabled white southerners to develop a unique, highly developed culture. Therefore, slavery enabled civilization to advance.[156]

AFRICANIZATION OF THE LABOR FORCE

These racist ideas became prevalent in the Chesapeake in the eighteenth century as planters transformed themselves into masters and primarily white indentured servants were replaced by black slave labor.[157] More and more advertisements prominently noted that the slaves being sold in the tidewater were coming not from the West Indies but directly from Africa.

In 1752, Benjamin Tasker Jr. and his brother-in-law Christopher Lowndes advertised in the *Maryland Gazette* that they were selling a cargo of slaves brought from the coast of Africa by Captain James Lowe on the *Elijah*.[158] In 1760, Thomas Ringgold and Samuel Galloway sold slaves brought from Angola aboard Captain John Wilkinson's *Jenny*.[159] In 1767, John Ridout and Daniel of St. Thomas Jenifer sold slaves in Annapolis who had been brought from the River Gambia.[160]

Between 1750 and 1773, Maryland planters purchased 6,841 slaves. Over 90 percent of them came directly from Africa—most from Senegambia and what is present-day Nigeria.[161] Local planters usually bought this labor—one or two at a time—at their own tobacco landings all around the bay.[162] Slavers also sold larger groups of slaves in Chestertown, Baltimore Town and Annapolis. The trade was quite lucrative. Slaves could be purchased on the African coast for between four and six pounds per head and then sold in the Chesapeake for as much as forty pounds.[163]

"Maryland's chief slave-selling entrepreneurs" in the eighteenth century were Thomas Ringgold and Samuel Galloway.[164] Thomas Ringgold and his brother William were Chestertown merchants; Samuel Galloway was their Annapolis partner. Ringgold & Galloway sold slaves on both sides of the bay, from the top of the Chesapeake to the Virginia tidewater. Even George Washington used their services. Sam Galloway often held his auctions in the Middleton Tavern near the dock in Annapolis.[165]

THE CONDITIONS OF SLAVE LIFE

Since labor defined the slaves' existence, when, where and how slaves worked generally determined the course of their lives.[166] While work on large plantations differed from work on small family farms, in both cases, the Plantation Revolution marked a sharp deterioration in the conditions of slave life.[167] As the domination of large plantation owners grew and more of their workforce came directly from Africa, all slaves came to have higher and higher levels of discipline, harsher working conditions and greater exploitation than ever before.[168]

Owners no longer worked in the fields. The first generations of slaves (seventeenth-century ones) had often slept and eaten under the same roofs as their owners.[169] Few planters had owned more than one or two laborers, and most had worked in the fields with them. The Plantation Revolution meant owners had dozens of slaves, and slaves lived in a world apart from their owners. Eighteenth-century owners withdrew from the fields and hired overseers; slaves became little more than "units of production."[170]

With the decline in the number of white indentured servants, slaves could no longer expect the working standards established for English servants. In the eighteenth century, slaves worked under closer supervision. They were expected to work more days and longer hours. Saturday became a full workday, and some slaves had to work on Sunday. Holidays were reduced to Christmas and Easter. Midday break time was reduced, and the workday was extended into evening. By the time slaves had come from their long day's work and fixed something to eat, there was little time for rest. One Eastern Shore slave said that his owner was trying "to make one man do the work of two."[171]

The level of violence dramatically increased in the eighteenth century, and slave owners invented new punishments beyond the rod, the lash or the fist.[172] Some slaves were branded as if they were cows or pigs. Overseers were hired who had reputations for "breaking slaves." Some took great pleasure in whipping slaves until their naked backs were covered with blood. Some whipped one slave at the beginning of each workday to remind all the other slaves what was awaiting them if they did anything to displease the overseer.[173]

Frederick Douglass cited one particularly horrible example of this violence on the Eastern Shore. One day in Talbot County, on Edward Lloyd's plantation, a young slave named Denby offended overseer Austin Gore. The overseer flogged the slave. After a few whacks, Denby broke away. He plunged into a nearby creek and refused to come out. Gore said he was going to count to three, and if Denby did not come out, Gore would shoot him. Then, Gore called, "One, two, three." When Denby did not move, Gore raised his gun and shot Denby through the head. The overseer explained to Colonel Lloyd that Denby had become unmanageable and without Gore's prompt action, order on the Lloyd plantation would be destroyed. While Gore had committed murder, he was never tried for any crime.[174]

It also became harder for slaves to form families and have independent lives. Chesapeake planters imported male and female slaves disproportionately, at a ratio of more than two males to every female.[175] Women were used in the fields just like men, with no regard for pregnancy, and female slaves had no protection against licentious overseers and slaveholders. Owners were not interested in slave families. They often split them up on separate plantations or sold away parts of families, and children were separated from their mothers when they were very young.[176] Owners also encouraged division among their slaves—house slaves versus field slaves, lighter-colored slaves versus darker slaves and the black overseer versus all the others.[177]

The slaves' independent economy of earlier years was ended. Now, all the slaves' time belonged to the owner—no truck farming or selling fish or raising a pig to make a little money. If the owner was in a slack time, he often hired his slaves out and collected the pay. Since there was now no way to earn money, there was now no way to buy freedom.[178]

As time went on, color became the key factor in discrimination. Plantation owners "redefined the meaning of race, investing pigment—both white and black—with a far greater weight in defining status than heretofore."[179] Negroes, mulattoes and Indians now were all grouped together into a single outcast group.[180]

People in England long had shown contempt for the poor—the inarticulate lower classes.[181] In the colonial Chesapeake, that contempt for the lower class was now directed toward all people of color. And all the negative character traits attributed to the poor more and more became the exclusive heritage of blacks. Blacks were considered to be ungrateful, irresponsible, lazy, dishonest and ignorant.[182] Anthony Johnson, whom we met in the first chapter, would not have recognized this eighteenth-century world.

Slavery, of necessity, rested on force.[183] While seventeenth-century slaveholders had petitioned the courts when they wanted to discipline their slaves, planters in the first half of the eighteenth century ruled their plantations like absolute sovereigns.[184] And they were backed by the power of the state. William Green, an Eastern Shore runaway, later wrote that the master had "all the power over the poor panting slave, and let him treat him as he will. The slave has no power to lay his grievance before any human being."[185]

Planters made the laws (they controlled the legislature); planters meted out justice (they were the judges on the courts); and, all the while, they asserted their natural right to rule.[186] Masters' authority radiated from the plantation not only to the statehouse and the courtroom but also to the church.[187] Men who wielded the whip during the week were church deacons or even ministers on Sunday. Frederick Douglass said of the latter: "For of all slaveholders with whom I have ever met, religious slaveholders are the worst. I have ever found them the meanest and basest, the most cruel and cowardly, of all others."[188]

While at times the slave owner's power was awesome, it should be noted, however, that that power was never absolute.[189] Slaves "fought back" in their own way—by slowing the pace of labor, doing shoddy work, intentionally misunderstanding instructions, breaking tools, truancy and, of course, by running away.[190]

THE DEGRADATION OF BLACKS

For all slaves in the eighteenth century, there was a constant. The whole system of slavery was designed to impress upon these laborers their inferiority and to undermine their humanity.[191] This degradation and humiliation began with names.[192]

Slaves in Maryland during the first thirty years of its settlement generally had names like Anthony Johnson, Francisco Menendez or Henry Matney. They married and established families. Many were baptized. They traveled throughout their communities and participated in the local economy. They used the courts and petitioned the legislature.[193]

Slaves who came into the Maryland colony after about 1660 seldom had more than one name.[194] They were Frank, or Tom, or Nell, or Harry. Owners stripped slaves of their identity by renaming them.[195] (In the television series *Roots*, Kunta Kinte is given the name "Toby" by the mistress of the plantation, even though he insists that he already has a name.)

Owners might rename their slaves with biblical names like Abraham, Isaac or Hagar or sarcastically call them by the names of ancient leaders, like Caesar or Cato, or even gods like Hercules. Slaves were given names more appropriate for barnyard animals—Bossy or Jumper. Sometimes an advertisement for a runaway made the slave seem like a pet animal. It might read, "a slave who answers to the name of Cuffey." Often, the most insignificant on the plantation were given the greatest names.[196]

From wills, inventories and land records, I know the names of seventy-six slaves who were owned by my ancestors on Hoopers Island during this

SLAVE NAMES IN MARYLAND

1634–1660	After 1660
Anthony Johnson	Frank, Tom, Nell, Harry
Francisco Menendez	Abraham, Isaac, Hagar
Henry Matney	Caesar, Cato, Hercules
	Bossy, Jumper, Cuffey

CHART 3. SLAVE NAMES IN MARYLAND, 1634–1660 AND AFTER 1660.

period. Of the seventy-six, only two have double names, and those are "Harry Boy" and "Patuson Tom." None have normal surnames.[197]

And it was not just names that degraded slaves. Slaves were not told their birthdays. When Frederick Douglass wrote his autobiography in 1845, he began his tale by saying that he did not know his age. He wrote:

By far the larger part of the slaves know as little of their ages as horses know of theirs, and it is the wish of most masters within my knowledge to keep their slaves thus ignorant. I do not remember to have ever met a slave who could tell of his birthday. They seldom came nearer to it than planting-time, harvest-time, cherry-time, spring-time, or fall-time.[198]

Later, birthdays became very important for slaves. Some slave owners promised to free slaves when they reached a certain age, for example thirty years old. When the time came for the slave to be freed, however, somehow he or she had miraculously gotten younger.[199] But the slave had no proof that he was old enough to be free.

Of course, birthdays were not the only things that slaves were not supposed to know. Most of all, if their father was white, they were not supposed to be concerned about who he was.

"Genealogical trees do not flourish among slaves," Frederick Douglass wrote.[200] He explained that it was "whispered" that his master was his father. But he did not know if that was correct because he was separated from his mother when he was an infant and never had an opportunity to ask her.[201] He did not know that he had brothers and sisters until his grandmother took him to Wye House when he was about seven years old.[202]

I know the names of my parents, grandparents, great-grandparents and beyond. That is because there are records of these people—birth certificates, death certificates, family Bibles, land records, wills, inventories and tombstones. There were few such records for slaves.

Then, there was the humiliation that was enacted by the government. Look at some of the laws passed by the slave owners who controlled the Maryland Assembly.[203]

In 1695, an act was passed that required any slave going from one of his owner's plantations to another to carry "a tickett or certificate" signed by his owner that gave the slave permission to move about.[204] This act was similar to one mentioned in the previous chapter that had referred to all servants and had not used the word *slave*. In 1704, this law was modified to equate a slave who had no pass and was more than ten miles from his master's house with being a runaway.[205]

In 1727, the Maryland government paid slave catchers to round up slaves who were running away to live with the Indians (five pounds for each runaway).[206] For the first offense, the runaway had one ear cut off; for the second offense, the other ear was cut off and the runaway was branded on the chin with the letter "R." If runaways were not reclaimed by their owners, the government sold them.[207]

In 1729, the General Assembly enacted a law "for the more effectual Punishment of Negroes, and other Slaves" that stated that if a Negro, or other slave, was guilty of having committed murder, treason or arson, the punishment would be

> to have the right Hand cut off, to be hang'd in the usual Manner, the Head severed from the Body, the Body divided into Four Quarters, and Head and Quarters set up in the most publick Places of the County where such Fact was committed.[208]

In 1737, the General Assembly thought it needed even stricter laws for slaves—"to keep them in Proper Bounds & Due order." So it enacted a law that if a slave was convicted of consulting, advising or conspiring to rebellion or if a slave was convicted of raping a white woman, the punishment was death without the benefit of clergy. And the government paid the slave owner compensation for his dead convicted slave.[209]

In 1752, the General Assembly passed legislation that forbade manumission "by any last Will or Testament" or the manumission of disabled and elderly slaves. Slaves could be freed only by deed and then only if they were "sound in body and mind, capable of labor and not over fifty years of age." Manumission was also illegal if the grant was written in part "during the last fatal illness of the master" or if the freeing of slaves affected the ability of creditors to settle their claims against the estate of the deceased.[210]

As the eighteenth century wore on, plantation blacks in colonial Maryland came to be treated less and less like human beings and more and more like commodities. Slaves became just another form of chattel—part of a person's movable property.

Three documents in the Dorchester County land records that concern my own ancestors vividly illustrate this idea of chattel. When Matthew Travers sold a number of items to his son-in-law Charles Nutter in 1737, the bill of sale read:

> *I the said Matthew Travers of Dorchester County…for and in Consideration of Fifty Pounds Current Money of Maryland…do give grant deliver and confirm unto the said Charles Nutter one Negro Woman called Hannah about Thirty years of Age and a Negro girl called Jhonah aged about four years old and four Cows and Calves and two year old Heifer and ten Head of Sheep and three head of Horses and five head of Hogs a Bed and Furniture.[211]*

To my ancestor, Hannah, Jhonah, a heifer and a bed were all the same type of thing. They were all simply his property.

Since slaves were property, they could be used as collateral when their owner wished to borrow money.[212] In 1813, one of my third-great-grandmothers used "my Negro Slave Polly" to secure a loan, promising to repay the debt within six months.

> *For the Consideration of the Sum of one hundred & seventeen Dollars Current money….I do hereby…deliver unto the said Jabus Travers my Negro Slave Polly…it being the true intent and meaning thereof that the said Negro is mortgaged by me the Said Elizabeth Travers to Secure to the Said Jabis Travers the payment of the money aforesaid.[213]*

When my seventh-great-grandmother Mary Hooper wrote her will in 1740, she left her grandsons "one half of a Negro woman named Fanny," as if this woman were a commodity that could be physically cut into pieces.[214]

Some people have made a comparison between the labor practices in New England factories in the early days of the Industrial Revolution and the labor system on southern plantations. But the two should never be confused with each other. White textile workers, no matter how poorly they were treated, were still persons—and they were free. Black slaves had become simply someone else's property.

CHANGES COME TO THE CHESAPEAKE

The Eastern Shore did not remain a slave society for very long. On most of the peninsula, by the time of the American Revolution, slaves had ceased to be essential to the economy.[215] Other parts of Maryland and much of the rest of the Upper South remained slave societies for much longer than the Eastern Shore.

Economic change came rapidly to the area in the second half of the eighteenth century. Tobacco could be grown on a field for only three years before the nutrients in the soil were exhausted, so farmers were continually clearing new fields for tobacco cultivation. Land on the Eastern Shore that was suitable for tobacco farming was in short supply.[216]

Tobacco gave way to mixed cultivation that combined tobacco with a variety of grains, corn and livestock. In the northern counties of the Eastern Shore in particular, farmers stopped growing tobacco altogether early on. By the late 1750s, Cecil, Kent and Queen Anne's (the three northernmost Eastern Shore counties) had become the colony's leading grain counties—producing wheat, flour and corn. In these counties, whites and blacks once again worked side by side.[217]

Economic change in the eighteenth century included the growth of towns and the construction of roads. And, as commercial activity began to move north, ports like Chestertown and Baltimore Town became far more important than the rural plantations on the lower Shore. Roads were being built throughout the colony. Chestertown benefitted from the construction. It was on the closest route from Philadelphia south. A ferry at Rock Hall, just west of Chestertown, connected the two shores of the bay.[218]

During the seventeenth century, the grain trade of the Chesapeake had been carried on largely by New England and West Indian vessels. In the first half of the eighteenth century, however, the local merchant marine grew and an increasing proportion of the West Indies trade began to be carried by Chesapeake-built and Chesapeake-owned vessels. Shipbuilding was concentrated on the Eastern Shore, especially in Kent and Talbot Counties. The white oak of Dorchester County was highly sought after for shipbuilding, so timbering became an important economic activity in that county.[219]

Ships built on the Eastern Shore sailed to both Atlantic ports like Charles Town (shown here) and the West Indies. *Courtesy of the Library of Congress.*

Export trade to the West Indies became centered on the Eastern Shore, particularly at Chestertown. In the 1770–75 period, grain shipments from that port averaged 130,000 bushels of wheat, 5,000 barrels of flour and 50,000 bushels of corn a year.[220] Many of the bay vessels were too small to engage in the oceanic tobacco trade. But they were perfect for taking grain, cattle and timber down the Atlantic coast to the West Indies, where they obtained rum, sugar, molasses, salt and slaves in exchange.[221]

In the eighteenth century, there also was a realignment of the labor force. At first, skilled labor was reserved for white non-slaveholders. Free and servant white men became artisans. Women (often the wives of these artisans) did weaving and dairying. With urbanization and growth of manufacturing and shipbuilding, the demand for artisans and laborers outstripped the number of available white workers. White employers, therefore, increasingly were forced to "put aside their racial prejudices" and employ slaves in these industries.[222] By the time of the American Revolution, only seven in ten male slaves in the Chesapeake tidewater worked in the fields.[223]

As planters diversified, year-round labor was no longer required of their slaves, and the practice of renting out slaves developed.[224] A new occupation developed—that of a broker, or jobber. This person's role was to connect slave owners and slaves with jobs, prepare the contracts and collect the money. Eventually, the "hiring business" became almost as organized as the slave trade.[225]

And a part of the realignment of labor had to do with the growth of the free black population. We will explore that big change in chapter three.

All these economic changes had a big impact on the Eastern Shore. First, they altered the traffic patterns on the Chesapeake. As Maryland shifted from an economy dependent on tobacco to one based on grain, commercial activity began to move north, away from the lower Chesapeake. And as more shipping traveled north to south along the bay (instead of east to west), that waterway became a barrier rather than a bond between the two Maryland shores. That water barrier, in turn, contributed to the growing isolation of the lower Eastern Shore. Northern counties became much more important than Talbot, Dorchester, Somerset and Worcester. And while ports like Chestertown and Baltimore Town prospered, southern Shore towns like Oxford declined.

The contact that Eastern Shore planters once had with the rest of the world became more and more limited.[226] When they no longer grew tobacco, interaction with men who regularly traveled to London, Amsterdam and Paris happened infrequently. So, the Shore became more parochial.[227] And the isolated, ethnically homogeneous, rural white population there had no interest in reducing the separation between black and white.[228] The attitudes they had formed about blacks during the Plantation Revolution would last for generations.

The impact of economic change on the Eastern Shore slave population was also significant. In this period, slaves took on new jobs. They became active on the waters of the bay as sailors and cooks. Many were employed in shipyards and in the timber industry. Some became blacksmiths, carpenters and shoemakers.[229] But in general, Eastern Shore slaves did not have their lives improved when their owners became more isolated and parochial. And the status of many was becoming more tenuous.

While those growing tobacco worked year-round, mixed farming required steady work only during the planting and harvesting seasons. For the remainder of the year, laborers had little to do with the crop, so planters scrambled to keep their slaves profitably occupied. This slack time contributed greatly to the sense of excess labor and the need to reduce the number of slaves.[230]

THE ROLE OF QUAKERS

In addition to the economic changes that came to the Chesapeake in the second half of the eighteenth century, there were also social and philosophical changes. Even before the War for Independence, some people in America were questioning the institution of slavery on ethical and religious grounds. That was true on the Eastern Shore among the Quakers.

The Religious Society of Friends was founded in England in 1652 by George Fox, with the main ideas of equality, simplicity, brotherhood and peace. Within a few years of its founding, Quakerism was introduced to Maryland's Eastern Shore. Soon after settlement was allowed there, ministering Friends traveled to the area and held meetings at Kent Island and in Talbot County.[231]

George Fox came to Maryland and preached to large crowds on both the Eastern and Western Shores. He had first seen slavery when he visited Barbados. He

George Fox (1624–1690). *Courtesy of the Library of Congress.*

spoke against slavery's excesses and urged slave owners to "train up their negroes in the fear of God, to use them mildly and gently, and after certain years of servitude to set them free."[232]

By the time George Fox came to the Eastern Shore, there were already four Quaker meetinghouses in Talbot County.[233] The clapboard Third Haven Meetinghouse was built in 1684. It still stands off South Washington Street in Easton. It is the earliest positively dated building in Maryland.[234]

Some settlers disliked Quakers because Quakers refused to serve in the military and they kept their hats on in court. In Virginia, a number of harsh laws were passed from 1659 to 1663 that were designed to forbid Quakers from entering the state, living in the state or holding worship services in the state.[235] This persecution led many Quakers to cross the border into Maryland, where freedom of religion was the accepted practice under Lord Baltimore. Many came to Somerset and Worcester Counties from Accomack and Northampton Counties on the eastern shore of Virginia.[236]

From about 1674 onward, a number of Maryland Quakers freed their slaves by wills or deeds of manumission.[237] This early interest in manumission, however, appears to have ended about 1710. Quaker families that held slaves continued to do so, and those who did not think the practice acceptable did not hold slaves.[238] Then, in the third quarter of the eighteenth century, that rather laissez-faire attitude among Quakers changed.[239]

In the spring of 1766, John Woolman, an itinerant Quaker "reformer," made the first of his three "walking journeys" through Talbot County to awaken the consciences of Eastern Shore Quakers. He wore undyed clothing to make a statement against the slave labor that was used in making dyes, and he went on foot to somewhat identify with the lives of slaves working in the fields—tired, thirsty, hot and sweating—to "feel their Condition," he said. Woolman traveled from slave owner to slave owner in the Quaker community, challenging Friends to free their slaves. He stressed that it was only the love of comfort, leisure and selfish profit that enabled them to hold their fellow man in bondage.[240]

After Woolman's "walking journeys," manumissions began to follow. Since slaves were considered property, all transactions dealing with them

Third Haven Meetinghouse, Easton, Maryland, 2017. *Courtesy of James D. Hedberg.*

were recorded in the land records. The Talbot County land records show some of the Quaker manumissions that were made after Woolman's journeys.

In 1767, Joseph Berry freed Hannah and Abraham.[241] In April 1768, Benjamin Berry, Joseph's younger brother, freed his nine slaves—Joe and Edward, Lucy and Rachel and the others.[242] Three weeks later, Elizabeth Neale freed all of her slaves.[243] These manumission papers make no mention of the cause for the owner's action. But two weeks before Berry made his manumissions, Daniel Adams in Dorchester County (which had a smaller Quaker population than Talbot) had freed two of his slaves (Rose and Pleasant), saying that he did this "more Especially to satisfye my Conscience relative to keeping of Slaves."[244] Few slave owners, however, copied the examples of these Quakers.

THE AMERICAN REVOLUTION

While the economy was changing on the Eastern Shore, political issues were becoming more important throughout the colonies. They were on the road to revolution and separation from Britain.

After the British won the French and Indian War, they left ten thousand British soldiers in America as a security force. The colonists were expected to pay for this defense, and to that end, Parliament passed a series of taxes that the colonists refused to pay. The colonists also questioned Parliament's right to levy such fees.[245]

Soon after the Stamp Act was passed in 1765, court officials in Maryland and elsewhere began issuing papers without stamps, in violation of the law, and citizens began a boycott of British goods.[246] Britain repealed the Stamp Act in 1766, not so much because of the colonists' complaints but because of pressure from British merchants who were being financially hurt by the colonists' boycott.

The British still expected the colonists to pay for their own defense. At the same time that Parliament repealed the Stamp Act, it passed a Declaratory Act that stated both that the colonies were subordinate to the Crown and Parliament and that colonial statutes could be struck down whenever the London government found them unacceptable.

The following year, the Townshend Acts were passed, imposing duties on all glass, lead, painters' colors, tea and paper imported into the colonies. In

Colonists protest the Stamp Act.
Courtesy of the Library of Congress.

1770, when British customs officials tried to collect those duties from John Hancock's sloop *Liberty,* the people of Boston roughed up the officials. From that point, trouble escalated. The governor called for two regiments of British soldiers to protect the customs officials. Boston's citizens snowballed the redcoats, and snow-balling degenerated into a mob attack. Someone fired, and four Bostonians died. Among the dead was a mulatto seaman named Crispus Attucks. His father was an African-born slave; his mother, a Native American.

The British repealed the Townshend duties except on tea. They thought the three-pence-per-pound tax would show the colonists who was boss. For three years, on the surface, relations remained generally calm. Then, in 1773, Britain gave the East India Company a monopoly on all tea sold to the colonies. The company decided to sell the tea through its own agents, a practice that did not sit very well with colonial merchants. In Charles Town, tea was landed but not allowed to be sold; in Philadelphia and New York, the tea was sent back to England.

A romanticized view of the
Boston Tea Party. *Courtesy of the
Library of Congress.*

In Boston, on December 16, 1773, a band of men painted like Mohawk Indians boarded the British ships and dumped the tea into the water. Parliament closed the Port of Boston to punish Massachusetts. The colonists reacted to that by sending representatives to the first Continental Congress in Philadelphia.[247]

The following autumn in Maryland, the *Peggy Stewart* arrived in Annapolis from London. Her cargo included two thousand pounds of tea. The owner of the ship, Antony Stewart, paid all the taxes due, including the hated tax on tea. Marylanders were irate. They told him that if he did not burn his ship with all its cargo, his house and family would be in danger. Stewart bowed to the mob and burned his ship.[248] Lexington and Concord followed in the spring of 1775. The American War for Independence had begun.

BLACKS IN THE AMERICAN REVOLUTION

Many blacks saw the American Revolution as an opportunity to fight for greater freedom and more civic participation. About five thousand were soldiers in the Revolutionary War. Most of them were from the North; most of them were free.[249]

One-fifth of the Patriot army in the northern colonies was black. (The New England colonies actually promised freedom to any slave who was willing to serve in the army.) Rhode Island had a segregated black regiment of 88 slaves with white officers. It was the only state to have such a unit. By mid-1778, there were about 755 black regulars in George Washington's Continental army—out of about 13,000 troops.[250]

Maryland was the only southern state to authorize slave enlistments.[251] In October 1780, the Assembly ordered that any able-bodied slave might be accepted as a recruit with his master's consent. In 1781, free blacks in Maryland became subject to the draft. Blacks also were accepted as substitutes for soldiers who could afford to pay someone else to take their place, and blacks served as pilots on the bay for the Maryland navy.[252] In all, probably 250 Maryland blacks fought in the Revolutionary War; 95 were regulars in the Continental army serving in the Maryland Line.[253] The story of one of them describes that experience.[254]

Thomas Carney was born on the Eastern Shore in 1754. In 1777, when the British were preparing to land troops in the northern part of the Bay, George Washington requested that Maryland, Pennsylvania and Delaware provide 2,500 volunteers to back up the Continental army. Thomas Carney was among the overwhelming numbers of Eastern Shoremen, white and black, who volunteered.

Carney joined a militia unit from Caroline County, and he reached Washington's army in time to participate in the October 1777 Battle of Germantown—a Patriot defeat. In the spring of 1778, Carney enlisted in the regular army, becoming a soldier in Maryland's Seventh Regiment. Carney was over six feet tall and known for his strength. He must have made quite a picture on the battlefield.

Early in 1780, Washington sent the Maryland Line south to reinforce the troops defending Charles Town. Carney fought at Camden, South Carolina; Guilford Court House, North Carolina; and Fort Ninety Six and Eutaw Springs, both in western South Carolina. At the siege of Fort Ninety Six, he saved his commanding officer, Captain Perry Benson, who was seriously wounded, by carrying him from the field of battle to a surgeon's station. There, Carney collapsed from the heat and the weight of Benson.

Carney was discharged in 1783, receiving a bonus and a bounty of one hundred acres of land in Western Maryland. He probably sold the bounty, because we find him again in the 1810 and 1820 Censuses of Caroline County, living near Denton, where Carney made a living farming. Captain Perry Benson, the white officer whom Thomas Carney had saved, was from Talbot County. He and Carney remained friends for the rest of their lives.

Not all Eastern Shore blacks, however, fought for the Patriots. On November 7, 1775, Virginia's royal governor, Lord Dunmore, issued a dramatic proclamation, saying,

> *I do hereby further declare all indentured Servants, Negroes, or others (appertaining to Rebels) free, that are able and willing to bear arms, they joining his Majesty's troops.*

By December, three hundred blacks were in British uniform. Most came from the Chesapeake tidewater, escaping from riverside plantations in canoes and boats stolen from their masters.[255] Patriots referred to them as Lord Dunmore's "Ethiopian Regiment."[256] Dunmore used them to raid the Maryland and Virginia coast.[257] His black soldiers helped hundreds of slaves escape, sometimes the entire population of a plantation's slave quarter.[258] Former slaves who had been pilots and navigators and who knew the rivers and marshes of the bay were especially helpful to the British.

To many slaves in the Chesapeake, the Union Jack represented freedom.[259] In late August 1777, General William Howe sailed his 260-ship armada up the Chesapeake to assault Philadelphia. The armada's presence in Maryland waters caused the number of runaways to escalate.[260] Other slaves were thought to be plotting rebellion. One Eastern Shore Patriot wrote: "The insolence of the Negroes in this county is come to such a height that we are under a necessity of disarming them."[261]

In March 1781, the British made a raid on the Eastern Shore, plundering the plantation of Edward Lloyd. He lost £5,000 of "hard money" and seven slaves. A short time later, when the British raided Mount Vernon, seventeen slaves fled, including some of George Washington's most trusted artisans and house servants.[262]

With the help of the French navy, the colonists prevailed. On October 18, 1781, General Cornwallis surrendered. The war lingered on for a while on the seas, but it was essentially over.[263]

MANUMISSION AND FREEDOM SUITS

Before the Revolution, one of the common complaints of Americans was that we were "slaves" to Britain.[264] Thomas Paine, author of the famous pamphlet *Common Sense*, responded to that type of outcry. He wrote, "How can Americans complain so loudly of attempts to enslave them, while they hold so many hundreds of thousands in slavery?"[265]

Many agreed with Paine that slavery was incompatible with the ideals of equality, life, liberty and the pursuit of happiness expressed in the Declaration of Independence.[266] There was "a terrible contradiction" between fighting for freedom yet denying freedom to 17 percent of the nation's inhabitants. Luther Martin from Somerset County, one of Maryland's representatives to the Constitutional Convention, strongly opposed slavery and refused to ratify the Constitution, saying he thought it absurd that the United States would permit states to continue "the only branch of commerce which is unjustifiable in its nature and contrary to the rights of mankind."[267]

In 1777, Vermont barred both slavery and indentured servitude.[268] New Hampshire and Massachusetts also soon abolished slavery. In 1780, Pennsylvania legislated gradual emancipation, calling slavery "disgraceful to any people, and more especially to those who have been contending in the great cause of liberty themselves."[269] In 1787, the Northwest Ordinance was passed, which prohibited slavery (except as punishment for crimes) in the territory that would become Ohio, Indiana, Illinois and Michigan.[270] By the first years of the nineteenth century, every state north of the Chesapeake had enacted some plan for emancipation.[271]

In Maryland, legislators were not ready to end slavery, but they did remove a rule that had been in force since 1752 and allowed manumission by properly executed deed or by will "at any time." The rights of creditors did have to be protected, and the slaves being freed could not be over fifty years of age and had to be able to work to support themselves at the time they were freed.[272]

In 1796, that law was amended to restrict manumissions to slaves under the age of forty-five. At the same time, the law levied an $800 fine against anyone who enslaved a free black or who made a slave who had a time limit to serve into a "slave for life."[273] Slave owners who were influenced by the egalitarian spirit of the times but who did not want to take the economic loss that freeing their slaves would bring often allowed their slaves to purchase their freedom.[274]

The idealism of the times certainly is obvious in Maryland manumission documents from the post–Revolutionary War period.[275] From 1787 to 1826, there were over 150 manumission papers filed in Dorchester County alone, which granted freedom to over three hundred slaves. In 1790, my third-great-grandfather Levin Parker freed Nell, one of his female slaves (aged thirty), and her children Daniel (aged ten), three-year-old Jacob and one-year-old Abram, stating that he found "it oppressive to holde Negroes in bondage."[276] A month later, Thomas Hill Airey of Dorchester County freed thirty slaves, saying:

> *Being conscious to myself that freedom and liberty is the unalienable right and privilege of every person born into the world and that the practice of holding Negroes in perpetual Bondage is…inconsistent with the strict rules of Justice and Equity.*[277]

In June, Thomas Beard freed his slaves Ben, Pug, Beththana, Jamie, Liddy and Stephen because he believed "it to be inconsistent with pure Christianity and natural Justice to hold a fellow Creture in bondage and slavery who has not by his crime forfeited his title to freedom."[278]

On Hoopers Island, on July 23, 1798, Thomas Bishop was freed. (Thomas Bishop's descendants lived next door to my maternal grandparents.) His manumission document reads:

> *Be it remembered that the following Manumission was Recorded on the twenty fourth day of October Seventeen hundred and ninety eight, to wit:*
>
> *To All whom these Presents shall come Greeting WE Henry Hooper & Henry Matney of Dorchester County and State aforesaid for diverse good causes and considerations, us thereunto moving, do hereby declare free manumit and Enfranchise, our negro man named Thomas Bishop, aged about Thirty five years, hereby Acknowledging the said negro discharged from all Claim of service and right of Property whatever from us our heirs executors and Administrators, Witness our hands and Seals this twenty third day of July In the year of our Lord one thousand seven hundred and ninety eight.*[279]

Thomas Bishop's "freedom papers" say that he is "free manumit and Enfranchise." He is not only free. He has the right to vote.

Constitutions written after the Revolutionary War reflected a spirit of egalitarianism. The Maryland Constitution of 1776 allowed adult male whites and free blacks to vote for the Lower House of the Legislature. In

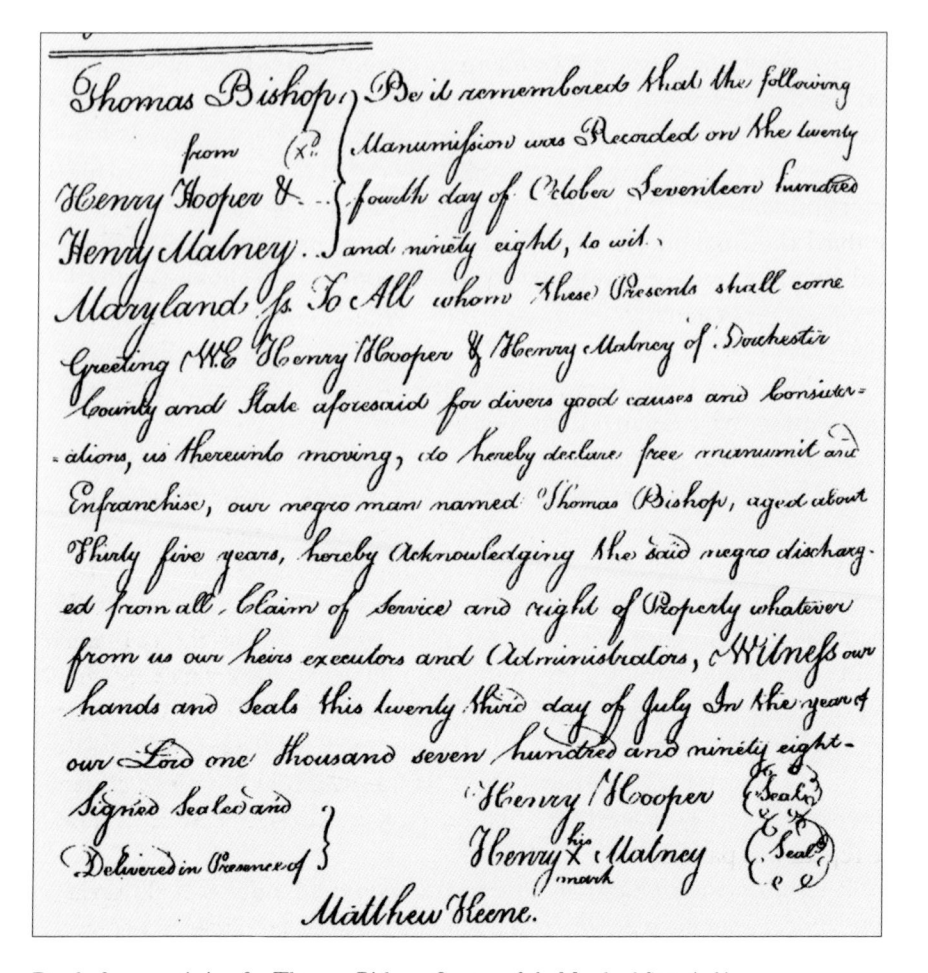

Deed of manumission for Thomas Bishop. *Courtesy of the Maryland State Archives.*

1792, Thomas Brown, a free black veteran of the war, ran for the House of Delegates from Baltimore.[280] Free black men could vote not only in Maryland but also in eight other states—Vermont, Connecticut, New Jersey, Pennsylvania, Delaware, North Carolina, Kentucky and Tennessee.[281] Thus, newly emancipated blacks in these jurisdictions were citizens of both their individual states and of the United States.

In addition to increased manumissions, the post–Revolutionary War also saw a plethora of freedom suits in Maryland's courts. Remember that one unique thing about slavery on the North American mainland was that children received their legal status from their mothers (not from their fathers). If a slave could prove to be descended from a white woman, the slave would be freed. Slaves in the post-Revolutionary period flooded the courts with their petitions, hoping to be helped by the new atmosphere of the times.[282] One example of these freedom suits is the Butler case.[283]

Eleanor Butler, who was commonly called "Irish Nell," was a white servant indentured to William Boarman, a friend of Charles Calvert, the third Lord Baltimore. In 1680, she decided to marry Charles, a slave. Lord Baltimore warned Nell that if she did this she would enslave both herself and her descendants. By the 1664 law that institutionalized slavery in Maryland, she would become a slave for as long as Charles lived, and their children would be slaves forever. But Nell supposedly insisted that she would "rather have Charles than your lordship."

The couple was married in a Catholic ceremony at William Boarman's home. They had seven or eight children, all of them born after the repeal of the sections of the 1664 law that applied to Nell and Charles.[284]

In 1770, William and Mary Butler, Nell's grandchildren, sued their owner Richard Boarman (William Boarman's grandson) for freedom on the basis that their grandmother was white. Maryland courts heard the case and allowed the testimony of elderly free blacks and whites who confirmed that Nell was indeed the ancestor of these two slaves. The Butlers won their liberty in the lower court, but the following year, the Court of Appeals reversed the decision. (The court ruled that the repeal of sections of the 1664 law did not apply to the Butlers since their marriage occurred before the repeal was passed.)[285]

Fifteen years later (after the American Revolution), one of Nell's great-grandchildren initiated another suit. After 1786, Maryland courts accepted both oral recollection and hearsay as evidence in such cases, increasing the chance that the slave's petition for freedom would be successful.[286] Mary Butler won her case. And so did many, many others.[287] In 1797, the Maryland attorney general complained, "Hundreds of negroes have been let loose upon the community by the hearsay testimony of an obscure illiterate individual."[288]

SLAVERY INCOMPATIBLE WITH RELIGION

In the post–Revolutionary War period, slavery was seen as being not only incompatible with the ideals of the Declaration of Independence but also incompatible with religion. Slavery violated both the unalienable rights of man and the Golden Rule.[289]

After the war, Quakers on the Eastern Shore picked up where they had left off in the 1760s. Increasingly, the discussion in Friends' meetinghouses turned to rejecting the practice of slavery as an official Quaker position.[290] Quakers like Joseph Berry and Benjamin Parvin from the Third Haven Meeting went to the western shore and testified to "the sweet sense of liberation which they had experienced in following the voice of 'the one true shepherd' and freeing themselves from the 'iniquitous' practice of holding their fellow man in bondage."[291]

In 1787, the Baltimore yearly meeting declared that slavery was wrong wherever men held others in bondage. And before long, the whole Quaker yearly meeting ruled that slaveholding was a "disownable offence." Slave owners would no longer be considered members, and money from them could not be accepted for Quaker work.[292] Some Quakers gave their freed slaves land, some gave them livestock and some gave them money. Some hired slaves they had freed and paid them the prevailing wages.

A group similar to the Quakers that flourished in Caroline County was the Nicholites (named for the Kent County, Delaware farmer Joseph Nichols). They spoke out against slavery as well.[293] Both of these groups became active in the Choptank Abolition Society (founded in Caroline County in 1790) and the Chester River Abolition Society. Both groups petitioned Congress to end the slave trade, and they hired lawyers to help slaves on the Shore with their freedom suits.

Presbyterians, Methodists and Baptists had similar ideas that slavery was contrary to Christian teachings. After the Revolutionary War ended, many people came under the influence of Methodist circuit riders like Francis Garrettson. Garrettson preached on the Eastern Shore that all mankind stood equal in God's eyes. The path to salvation, he said, lay open to everyone, black and white alike. At hundreds of camp meetings, Methodist and Baptist evangelicals made converts of unprecedented numbers of both whites and blacks.[294]

At Christmas time in 1784, Methodist ministers meeting at the Lovely Lane Church in Baltimore voted to formally separate from the Church of England. They also declared that slavery was "contrary to the golden laws of God," and they gave their members twelve months to liberate their slaves.[295]

We see these religious concerns in Eastern Shore manumission documents. Joseph Andrews of Dorchester County freed his slaves in 1787, saying:

> *being conscious to myself…that the practice of holding Negroes in perpetual slavery and Bondage is repugnant to the pure precepts of the gospel of our Lord Jesus Christ and Inconsistent* [with] *the strict rules of Justice and equity.*[296]

"Camp Meeting of the Methodists in N. America," 1819, M. Dubourg, engraver. *Courtesy of the Library of Congress.*

Thomas Hill Airey used much the same language as Andrews when he manumitted his slaves in 1790, but he added the phrase: "under a full assurance that if I continued to hold them in bondage I should never be received into that rest that remains for the people of God."[297]

This pious Eastern Shore Methodist was concerned for his own soul. He feared that as a slave owner he would never be accepted into Heaven.

MAKING ACCOMMODATIONS

In the end, however, idealism and threats of Hell were not enough. Many slave owners hedged their bets. They added specific dates to the time their slaves were to be freed, sometimes twenty years or more in the future. That way they seemed to soothe their conscience, while at the same time not denying themselves the benefits of their slaves' labor.

Joseph Andrews freed his slaves, but added: "my intent is that females serve and their increase born in the time of their slavery till they are thirty-five years of age."[298] Thomas Hill Airey freed all thirty of his slaves, giving a very precise timeline for their freedom:

Titus and Rose to be free immediately. Judah, Peter, Harry, Nan, Isaac, Leenah, Hetty, Lina, Daphne, Flora, and Charlotte to be free the first day of January next [1791]. Jim to free January 1st 1796. George and John to be free January 1st 1797. Rose to be free January 1st 1792. Matthew to be free January 1st 1799. Rachel to be free January 1st 1795. Henny to be free January 1st 1795. Patience to be free January 1st 1797. Nel to be free January 1st 1800. Nathan to be free January 1st 1802. Sampson and Levin to be free January 1st 1803. Sidney to be free January 1st 1804. Peg to be free January 1st 1805. Tilly to be free January 1st 1806. Joseph to be free Jan'ry lst 1810. Jesse to be free January 1st 1811.

Only two of Airey's slaves (Titus and Rose) were immediately free. Jesse would not be free until 1811; he would be enslaved for twenty-one more years.[299]

Slave owners also promised freedom contingent on good behavior or that, during their term, slaves never misbehave or try to run away. "Contingency manumission" was a common weapon in managing slaves on the Eastern Shore.[300] In 1808, John Braughan freed eight slaves and any children they might have according to a schedule of dates. But delayed manumission was not enough. He added to the manumission document the statement: "I do further observe that if them or either of theire children which is under servitude shall be out of there Owners Imploy by Runaway or being absent, when apprehended they shall be bound to make up all lost time."[301]

So, their terms would no longer be in effect.

Thomas Lockerman freed seven of his slaves in 1824 according to specific dates and then added:

and it is hereby made the express Condition of the above Manumission that if the above named Negroes…or any other person for them shall petition any legal Authority for their freedom before the different terms of Servitude aforesaid shall Expire then this deed of Manumission shall be null and void and the one so petitioning shall be and remain a slave for life.[302]

No freedom suits for any of Lockerman's slaves. "Term slavery" and "contingency manumission" robbed Eastern Shore slaves of their most productive years.[303]

And the church made accommodations, too. At first, Presbyterians and Baptists condemned the institution of slavery as inconsistent with the law of God, but eventually, they let local churches make their own decisions about emancipation.[304] In 1796, the Methodist Conference condemned slavery but retracted its 1784 antislavery rule. Now you could keep your slaves and still be a member of the church.[305] In 1804, the conference went even further, ordering a separate *Discipline* (or set of bylaws) for its southern churches, with all the antislavery statements deleted.[306] Then, in 1845, Methodist and Baptist Churches formally divided over slavery, forming the Methodist Episcopal Church, South and the Southern Baptist Convention.[307]

Forced to defend their own moral standards, the southern clergy came up with new arguments. Slavery, they claimed, was biblical. The Apostle Paul recognized its existence in Roman society, and he did not denounce it. Furthermore, slavery was a civil institution outside the scope of the Church. By separating ecclesiastical issues from social and political affairs, the clergy did not have to deal with racial injustice.[308] And ministers began to preach from the letters of Saint Paul that slaves should obey their masters, promising them freedom and equality in heaven.[309] Only the Quakers remained committed to abolition.

The humanitarian ideas that came out of the euphoria of American independence—freedom and equality for all—did not last, and white racial attitudes remained unchanged.[310] The United States lost its chance to peacefully end the institution of slavery.

IN SUMMARY

In this chapter, we have examined approximately fifty years of history—the second half of the eighteenth century, when blacks on Maryland's Eastern Shore were greatly affected by two big revolutions.

During the Plantation Revolution, slaves became essential to the booming tobacco economy. Large plantation owners controlled the Assembly, the courts and the Church. The conditions of slave life sharply deteriorated, and planters transformed their slaves from human beings into chattel. Also during this period, Eastern Shoremen developed the attitude that color indicated inferiority. While the Plantation Revolution did not last long, that attitude remained.

In the American Revolution, Eastern Shore blacks fought in both the Patriot army and in Lord Dunmore's Ethiopian Regiment. Many Eastern

Shore slaves ran away during that time. After the Revolution, noting the contradiction between slavery and the principles of liberty and the Golden Rule, manumissions and freedom suits increased. But, these manumissions often came with terms or contingencies. Among religious groups, only the Quakers remained committed to abolition.

By the end of this period, abandoning tobacco to raise grain and livestock made much of the Eastern Shore no longer dependent upon slave labor. The area had reverted into a society with some slaves.

3

"SELLING SOUTH"

I n the second chapter, we saw that a labor-intensive tobacco economy did not last very long on the Eastern Shore of Maryland. By the late eighteenth century, major economic changes had come to the area. One of those changes was the realignment of labor. A part of that realignment had to do with the growth of the Shore's free black population.

AN EXPLOSION OF FREE BLACK POPULATION

Actually, the free black population on the Eastern Shore did not grow. It exploded. The spectacular increase in the number of free blacks came about because of manumission, successful freedom suits, self-purchase, natural increase and immigration.[311]

Consider these statistics:[312] In 1755 (two decades before the American Revolution), a Maryland census counted 1,817 free blacks. Half were under sixteen, and nine out of ten were mulatto.[313] Between 1755 and 1790 (post–Revolutionary War), that free black population grew by over 300 percent to 8,043.[314] And, by 1810, the free black population had risen to almost 34,000.

In 1790, Maryland had a total black population of over 111,000, but only about 7 percent were free. By 1810, however, almost one-quarter of all blacks in Maryland were free. Look at these statistics another way. In 1790, only 1 in 13 Maryland blacks was free. By 1810, the number was about 1 in every 4.[315]

MARYLAND'S FREE BLACK POPULATION
(% of total black population that was free)

1755	1,817 free blacks (4.0%)
1790	8,043 free blacks (7.2%)
1810	33,927 free blacks (23.3%)

CHART 4. MARYLAND'S FREE BLACK POPULATION, 1755–1810.

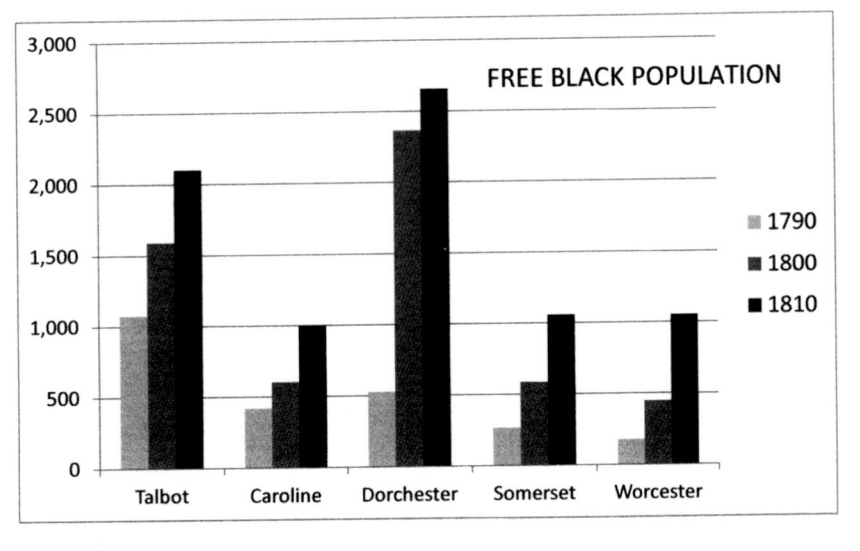

GRAPH 3. FREE BLACK POPULATION BY COUNTY, 1790–1810.

All the counties of the Eastern Shore showed this increase, especially the five counties of the Lower Eastern Shore: Talbot, Caroline, Dorchester, Somerset and Worcester. Talbot County's free black population doubled, from a little over 1,000 in 1790 to 2,103 in 1810. In Worcester County in 1790, there were only 178 free blacks. By 1810, however, over 1,000 lived there. That is a 500 percent increase.[316]

Dorchester County's numbers can help us even more clearly visualize this dramatic increase. The big explosion there came between 1790 and 1800 when there were many manumissions and successful "freedom suits." In 1790, there were 528 free blacks living in Dorchester County; by

1800, there were 2,365, giving Dorchester County the largest free black population of any county on the Shore. And the growth was to continue into the next decade.

THE REALITY OF THE INCREASED NUMBERS

On the Eastern Shore, as in much of the Upper South, free blacks and slaves were entwined in the same families, workplaces and churches.[317] Free blacks and slaves intermarried. (Of course, this often meant that the married couple only saw each other on Sundays.) Free blacks continued to reside with or near their former masters. A part of that was because planters often still owned the spouses and children of former slaves, seeing them as a lever to access the labor of free blacks. Some planters rented plots of land to former slaves. Having free blacks as tenants also guaranteed extra hands nearby during planting and harvest times.[318] Free blacks and slaves often shared the same workplaces. Farmers hired free blacks, and free and slave worked in the fields side by side. Free blacks and slaves also worked together in the timber industry and in shipbuilding.

After the Revolutionary War, tidewater blacks—free and slave—essentially turned themselves into African Americans.[319] Blacks of diverse backgrounds (whether they were of the Ibo, Ashanti, Congolese or Mandinka tribe) joined together to create African churches, especially the African Baptist Church and the African Methodist Episcopal Church. And they made African burial grounds. So free blacks and slaves shared the same churches and the same graveyards.[320]

Some free blacks became property owners and joined the middle class. As white farmers left the tidewater for opportunities in Kentucky and Ohio, free blacks on the Eastern Shore were at times able to purchase farmland at bargain prices.[321] In Talbot County, for example, there were eighteen free black property owners in 1793. By 1800 (just seven years later), that number had increased to eighty-eight.[322] Some of these free black property owners became slave owners as well.[323]

On Hoopers Island, on July 31, 1812, Levin Parker and his wife, Sarah, sold to "Thomas Bishop, negro" seven acres of a tract of land known as "Parker's Beginning." Four years later, Levin's son John W. Parker sold Bishop an additional six acres of the family tract and, in 1819, thirteen more acres.[324] The slave-owning Parkers apparently had no problem with enabling a free black to become their permanent next-door neighbor. That open-mindedness, however, was rare.

FROM CHATTEL SLAVERY TO CASTE SLAVERY

The egalitarian ideas of the Revolutionary years did not last very long. As the number of free blacks increased on the Eastern Shore, a two-caste system developed, with rigid divisions between black and white.[325] Freedom for blacks did not mean equality. And as quickly as the numbers of free blacks in the state increased, equally quickly lawmakers added more and more oppressive proscriptions to their lives—continually chipping away at their liberty and further distinguishing them from white people.[326] The objective was to keep free blacks "in their place."[327]

This discrimination is evident even in the early days of the republic. In 1790, the first Naturalization Law was passed. It restricted naturalization to "free *white* persons of good moral character." And in 1792, completely ignoring the important role played by black soldiers in the Revolutionary War, Congress formally excluded blacks from the military.[328]

After 1796, manumitted slaves in Maryland could not be elected to office. They could not give evidence against any white person. They could not testify in court cases in which slaves were petitioning for freedom.[329] And the right of free blacks like Thomas Bishop to vote for the Lower House of the Legislature was canceled on December 31, 1801, when the Maryland Constitution was amended to read, "Every free *white* male citizen of this state *and no other*...shall have the right of suffrage."[330] With each legislative session, new regulations were passed.[331]

By 1806, because "great mischiefs have arisen from slaves coming into possession of the certificates of free negroes," Maryland required free blacks to register with the local magistrate. They had to tell their name, sex, color, age, stature, any identifying marks they had and how they had been freed. Registration cost twenty-five cents and had to be renewed every three years for rural blacks and annually for urban ones. Failure to register resulted in a fine; default of the fine meant they could be sold back into slavery.[332]

The freed black's right of assembly was limited; free blacks were required to obtain a permit to own a dog, and they could not own guns.[333] Free blacks could not even sell corn, wheat or tobacco without a license.[334] Free blacks visiting Maryland after 1807 could stay no longer than two weeks. Then, when a delegate complained that "many beggarly blacks have been vomited upon us," the Maryland legislature prohibited the entry of all free blacks into the state.[335]

It was white racial prejudice that led to all these restrictions.[336] This letter written by a Marylander in 1818 tells the real truth:

Be their industry ever so great and their conduct ever so correct, whatever property they may acquire or whatever respect we may feel for their character,…we could never consent, and they could never hope to see… free blacks or their descendants visit our houses, form part of our circle of acquaintances, marry into our families, or participate in public honours or employment.[337]

SLAVERY IN THE POST-REVOLUTIONARY WAR PERIOD

It was not just the free black population that was growing in the Chesapeake during the Revolutionary wartime years. From 1775 to 1783, the slave population also increased. In 1770 (at the time of the Boston Massacre), Maryland had 63,818 slaves.[338] At war's end in 1783, the slave population had risen to about 83,000.[339] Most of the approximately 20,000 increase was indigenous. Slaves were now a self-producing labor force—a "human crop."[340]

Thomas Jefferson obviously understood this when he wrote:

I know of no error more consuming to an estate than that of stocking farms with men almost exclusively. I consider a woman who brings a child every two years as more profitable than the best man on the farm. What she produces is an addition to the capital, while his labor disappears in mere consumption.[341]

Charles Carroll of Annapolis was also aware of this economic benefit of being a slave owner. In a letter to his son Charles Carroll of Carrollton, he wrote: "I have taken a very Exact Acct [Account] of all the Negroes Here…. Negroes as pr [per] List taken Decr [December]: 1st: 1773—330. Do [ditto]: as pr List taken Decr: 1st: 1767—273. Increase in 6 years—57."[342]

That was almost a 21 percent increase in the number of slaves Carroll had on his plantations. That increase most likely occurred because of children born to female slaves that he already owned.

Frederick Douglass, in his autobiographies, wrote about Edward Covey, a poor Dorchester County farmer who was able to buy only one slave—Caroline. "Scandalous and shocking as is the fact," Douglas wrote, "he boasted that he bought her simply '*as a breeder*.'"[343]

After Mr. Covey bought Caroline, he hired a man from a neighboring farmer and put the man with Caroline every night. Some months later,

Caroline gave birth to twins. Douglass wrote: "At this addition to his human stock, both Edward Covey and his wife, Susan, were extatic with joy."[344]

This natural increase in the slave population at the end of the eighteenth century was tremendously important, because on many plantations, the number of slaves soon exceeded the number of workers that were needed.[345] That was especially true on the Eastern Shore as the tobacco economy declined.[346]

END OF THE AFRICAN SLAVE TRADE

In March 1807, at the request of President Thomas Jefferson, Congress passed an act ending the African slave trade on the first date that the Constitution allowed such a prohibition.[347] After January 1, 1808, it would "not be lawful to import or bring into the United States or the territories thereof from any foreign kingdom, place, or country, any negro, mulatto, or person of colour, with the intent to hold, sell, or dispose of such as a slave to be held to service or labour."[348]

The law was quite strong. U.S. citizens were forbidden to build, equip or finance slave ships. Doing so would result in a $20,000 fine and loss of the ship. A sliding scale of penalties was given for importing illegal slaves—fines from $1,000 to $10,000 and prison terms from five to ten years. Buying illegally imported slaves would result in an $800 fine per slave.[349]

Theoretically, the law meant that after January 1, 1808, all new slaves in the United States would be native-born. Their ancestors might have come from the West Indies or from Africa, but these new slaves would have no personal knowledge of any place other than America.[350]

But theory and practice are not the same things. The 1807 law provided that Africans caught up in the illegal trade would be treated according to the law of the state where they were found or brought to. That was fine, if they were found or brought to Maryland. Maryland had prohibited the African slave trade twenty-five years earlier in 1783, at the end of the Revolutionary War. Any African imported into Maryland as a slave after that date became free.[351] But if contraband slaves were found off the coast of a state like South Carolina, that state sold them and they ended up being enslaved anyway.

Additionally, there was so much money to be made that, in spite of the law, an illegal trade in slaves continued until the Civil War.[352] Dorchester County shipbuilders continued to build schooners and brigs for the African trade.

3404	Peru .... Thomas	3	88	1	7 m.	I.		1845	Camden, Me.	Rockland	Thomas			Bos. May '58
3405	Peruvian. T.Outhouse Top.	3	110	1	10 m.	I.		1846	Hopewell, N.S	St. Johns	T. Outhouse			NY. Feb. '59
3406	Peter Mowell .Small Sc.	2	129	1	9 o.	C. I	C Nov. '58	1855	Dorchester Md	New Orleans	Butler	6'	M	NO. Apr. '59
3407	Peter Ritter Cussman		120	1	7 s. c.	I.		1833	Connecticut	Hoboken	Vanbuskirk			NY. Apr. '59
3408	Petrel .... Gayle	2—	108	1	9 m.	I.		1852	La Have, N.S	Lunenburg	Rodenheiser			Apr. '58
3409	Petrel ..... Fitzgerald	2	129	1	10 m.	I.	Z Apr. '57	1850	Norfolk, Vir.	Baltimore	Fitzgerald	M	P.	Bal. Jan. '59
3410	Poytona. . J.T.Gilman	2½	93	1	9 m.	I.		1849	Belfast, Me.	Belfast	Lane		F.	NY. Apl. '59
3411	P. F. Williston	2	60	1	9 o.	C. I.		1848	Newburyport	Provincet'n	J. Small		F. x Cotta.	Bos. Mar '59
3412	P. G. Maddox	2½	73	1	8 o. c.	C. I.		1846	Southport	Southport	Maddox		F.	Nov '55
3413	Pharos ..... Robbins	2	65	1	9 m.	I.		1852	Camden, Me.	N. Bedford	Robbins		F.	NY. Apr. '59
3414	Pheasant ..... Daley	3	81	1	10 m.	I.		1847	Granville	Halifax	A. W. Corbitt		F. r 98.	Oct. '57

American Lloyd's Register 1859 Peter Mowell

The schooner *Peter Mowell* shown in a Lloyd's of London listing of insured ships. *Courtesy of James D. Hedberg.*

They also retrofitted existing ships to accommodate slave cargo. One example of that is an eighty-eight-foot, 129-ton schooner named the *Peter Mowell*.

According to the records of the British insurance company Lloyd's of London, the *Peter Mowell* was built of white oak in Dorchester County in 1855. At first, the ship carried cargo and farm goods up and down the East Coast. In 1858, the schooner was sold to Salvador Prats in New Orleans. (It had probably already been retrofitted for the slave trade.) On July 25, 1860, the boat went aground on Lynyard Cay in the Abaco Islands in the Bahamas. It was carrying four hundred slaves from the Congo River.[353]

Philip Curtin, a Hopkins historian and an expert on the slave trade, estimated that as many as fifty thousand slaves were brought into the United States from 1808 to 1860 as a result of the illegal trade.[354]

THE "SECOND MIDDLE PASSAGE"

With the end of the foreign slave trade nationwide, the legal trade in slaves within the United States did not die. Rather, it grew. The difference was that instead of most of the slave trade being international, it became internal. The Eastern Shore, the Chesapeake area as a whole and much of the rest of the Upper South became net exporters of slaves.[355] Some historians call this internal slave trade the "second middle passage."[356]

In 1800, nearly three-fourths of American slaves resided on the Atlantic Seaboard between the Delaware River and the Savannah River. So, 75 percent of all American slaves lived in what was called slavery's "heartland." But, the internal slave trade changed that arrangement. By 1820, that earlier 75 percent proportion had dropped to 60 percent—less than two-thirds. By

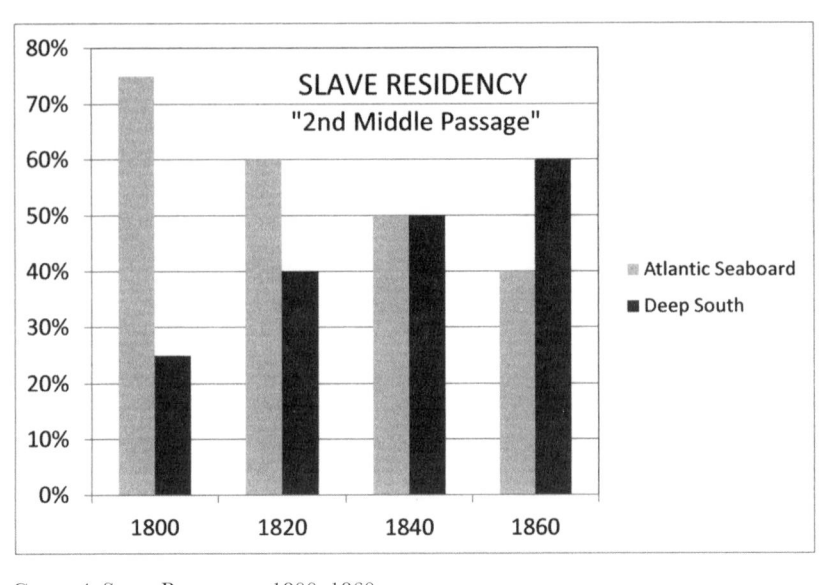

GRAPH 4. SLAVE RESIDENCY, 1800–1860.

1840, no more than half of America's slaves lived in what had once been slavery's heartland.[357]

Then, during the 1850s, nearly a quarter of a million slaves were moved from the seaboard to the interior, with more than half of that number being taken west of the Mississippi River. So, by 1860, the majority of the slave population—over 60 percent—resided in the Deep South, outside the seaboard slave states.[358]

The internal slave trade was a source of enormous profit for planters in the Chesapeake. Between 1780 and 1810, it is estimated that 115,000 slaves from the tidewater were "sold South."[359] But that lucrative trade was interrupted by war.

THE WAR OF 1812

In 1812, partly in response to Britain's annoying practice of pressing American sailors on the high seas, the United States declared war. The British blockaded the Chesapeake and made hit-and-run attacks all up and down the bay, raiding the region largely at will.[360] In April 1813, both George Town and Frederick Town on the Sassafras River were sacked and burned. Queenstown (just across Prospect Bay from the British base on Kent Island) was looted; St. Michaels on the Miles River was attacked twice.[361] On Slaughter Creek in Dorchester County, houses, boats and tobacco were torched.[362]

The British military had explicit orders not to incite a slave revolt, but they did accept slaves who ran away from their masters. Hundreds fled during the naval campaign of 1813. In November, Captain Robert Barrie wrote to Admiral Sir John B. Warren: "The Slaves continue to come off by every opportunity....Several Flags of Truce have been off to make application for their Slaves...but not a single black would return to his former owner."[363]

One of the first Eastern Shore slaves to seek asylum aboard a British warship was a Talbot County slave named Daniel Wright, a highly skilled shipyard worker who belonged to Francis Wrightson. Daniel had first escaped in 1808, and his owner believed that he had fled to Philadelphia. The British offered this fugitive an opportunity for freedom.[364]

In the War of 1812, the British had a manpower shortage in the Chesapeake.[365] In the Revolutionary War, Virginia's Governor Lord Dunmore had offered to free slaves who were willing to fight for the British. Vice Admiral Sir Alexander Cochrane, who was in command of the British

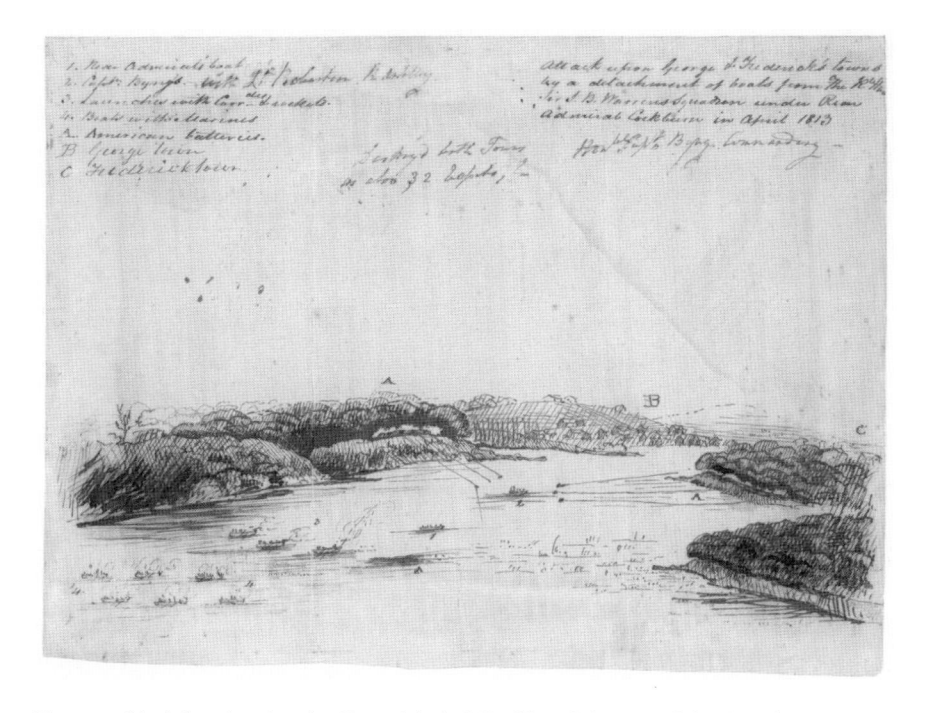

Topographical drawing showing Rear Admiral Cockburn's boats and the American batteries on either side of the Sassafras River, April 1813. *Courtesy of the Library of Congress.*

fleet in the bay, copied Dunmore's example. On April 2, 1814, he issued a proclamation in which he offered slaves a choice. They could either serve in the British military or be evacuated as free settlers to British possessions in North America or the West Indies.[366]

One thousand copies of Cochrane's proclamation were distributed throughout the tidewater area, and within four weeks, more than one hundred slaves had fled their plantations. (Actual pay, good food and decent clothing were strong recruiting incentives.) Black soldiers were trained at Fort Albion, the British base on Tangier Island in the lower Chesapeake. They were given arms and red-coated uniforms and formed into the Colonial Marines. Because they knew the local waterways and plantations, they played a part in almost every British landing party in the tidewater. Many also served with a squadron under Rear Admiral Sir George Cockburn that invaded Cumberland Island, Georgia, in December 1814. By the end of the war, the Colonial Marines included some three hundred former tidewater slaves.[367]

When the war was ended by the Treaty of Ghent on Christmas Eve 1814, the first clause of the treaty promised that Britain would return "any slaves or other private property" that it had taken. But Britain maintained that it had not "taken" any slaves. Rather, slaves had decided to flee. The issue was finally decided by the arbitration of Tsar Alexander I of Russia. He ruled that Britain was responsible for 3,582 slaves, for which Britain paid the United States over $1 million as compensation. Of those slaves, 714 came from Maryland. Their owners were awarded $280 for each slave lost in the war.[368]

KIDNAPPING ON THE EASTERN SHORE

It should be noted that when the war ended in 1815, few slaves worked in cotton fields and few slaves resided in the Deep South.[369] That was to change. Since the 1808 ban on the importation of slaves generally restricted the supply of slave labor to slaves who were already in the country, the value of those slaves skyrocketed. Advertisements for Eastern Shore runaways clearly show the money involved.

In 1783, the reward for Jonathan was $4. By 1833, Bill and Ambrose commanded $40 if taken in Talbot County, $60 if taken out of the county and $200 if captured out of state—that is, $100 each. By 1850, the average

Left: From the *Maryland Journal & Baltimore Advertiser*, July 8, 1783.

Right: From the *Commercial Chronicle & Daily Marylander*, June 1, 1833.

price for one fugitive slave was approaching $200.[370] And in some areas of the South, a healthy male slave was now worth $1,000. That kind of money was a great incentive for kidnappers.[371]

Notorious on the Eastern Shore was the Patty Cannon/Joe Johnson gang, which operated at the intersection of the borders of Dorchester County, Caroline County and the state of Delaware—a convenient legal no-man's land if someone was trying to evade the law.[372] Patty had a house about a quarter of a mile from the crossroads where the boundary lines all came together. She was described as a short, chunky woman with a large neck, coal-black hair and large black eyes (furtive, so they say). She was said to be as strong as an ox and swore like a seaman.[373] Joe Johnson, her son-in-law, was physically intimidating—six feet tall, mean and fearless.[374]

Joe Johnson built a tavern a short distance from Patty's house. It was about three miles from Cannon's Ferry, where people crossed the Nanticoke River. Passengers coming from the southern part of the Eastern Shore would be met at the ferry by stagecoaches coming from Cambridge. The tavern became a convenient place for them to stop.

Patty, Joe Johnson and other members of their gang hijacked free blacks and stole slaves all up and down the Eastern Shore and as far north as Philadelphia.[375] The attic of Joe's tavern was the gang's slave pen. The area was connected to the main floor with a stairway that was hidden in a closet.

Joe Johnson's Kidnappers Tavern as it appeared in 1883. From *The Entailed Hat* by "Gath" (George Alfred Townsend), illustrated edition, 1955. *Courtesy of the author.*

The kidnappers chained their victims in leg irons and, when they had a sufficient quantity, put them on schooners headed down the bay to Georgia.

In 1821, Patty, Joe Johnson and other gang members were indicted for kidnapping free blacks. Only Joe was found guilty; he was punished by having his ears nailed to the pillory and then given thirty-nine lashes.[376] In 1829, Patty Cannon was indicted on four counts of murder when bodies were found buried on her farm. She died in her cell in the Georgetown, Delaware jail—perhaps of self-inflicted poison.[377]

Patty Cannon and Joe Johnson were really small-time operators. Their activities were merely harbingers of what was to come when big business entered the slave trade.[378]

THE AMERICAN COLONIZATION SOCIETY

While many people opposed slavery and hoped that it would eventually die out, many of those same people could not picture living in a society with a large number of blacks who were free.[379] Slave owners, at the same time, objected to free blacks because their presence refuted the idea that black people were naturally inferior and therefore needed to be enslaved.[380]

After the War of 1812, one solution offered for what both abolitionists and slaveholders saw as the problem of increasing numbers of free blacks was the American Colonization Society, which was founded in 1816.[381] Local chapters were formed in many counties throughout Maryland, including Dorchester County and Queen Anne's County. The society's objective was to raise funds to pay for blacks to resettle in Liberia in West Africa.

In 1827, the American Colonization Society sought federal support. (By then, Maryland had the largest free black population of any state in the nation.) Maryland and all the rest of the northernmost tier of slave states (that is, the whole Upper South) supported the American Colonization Society's proposal. The cotton states, however, opposed it, with the Georgia legislature denouncing colonization as "a scheme to impoverish and depopulate the South."[382]

Picture distributed by the American Colonization Society showing a native village in Liberia. *Courtesy of the Library of Congress.*

Nat Turner's rebellion as portrayed in 1831. *Courtesy of the Library of Congress.*

Then, in 1831, in Southampton County, Virginia (west of Norfolk), a slave named Nat Turner led a revolt that resulted in the deaths of more than fifty whites. The revolt was soon put down, but Nat Turner was not captured until several weeks later, when he was discovered hiding in a field by a local farmer. Newspapers and broadsides of the time stirred up racial feelings by portraying the blacks who were involved in the revolt as violent murderers who cut down men, women and children indiscriminately. After this rebellion, whites throughout the slave-owning states became more fearful of other uprisings, and they passed more and more legislation restricting both blacks and whites. The rights of free speech, assembly and the press were increasingly curtailed. Mail coming from the North was routinely searched, as were suspicious travelers.[383]

The Maryland legislature passed new laws criminalizing routine black behaviors. Black education was prohibited, and white ministers were required to conduct all black worship services. Blacks could not travel without the consent of a county justice. Blacks could not operate a boat unless under the supervision of a white captain. Free blacks from other states could not come to Maryland to live, and they could not visit for longer than ten days.[384]

As of 1831, newly freed slaves were forbidden to remain in the state. So a free black could not buy his enslaved wife or children and free them. They had to remain his slaves or leave Maryland. (That is probably what we see in the 1840 Census, in which a number of free blacks have slaves in their households.)

In 1831, perhaps because of nervousness over the Nat Turner revolt, the Maryland legislature also set aside $20,000 to be used to repatriate free blacks who would be willing to resettle in Africa.[385] It set up "The State of Maryland in Liberia"—an independent country with its own code of laws.[386] The legislature ordered county clerks to report all manumissions to a state-appointed Board of Managers for the Removal of Colored People.[387]

In Cambridge, there was an American Colonization Society chapter with all black members. In 1851, the organization sent Thomas Fuller, a local barber, and Benjamin Jenifer, a minister, to Africa to inspect the colony. When the two returned to the United States, Fuller announced that he and his family were going to Liberia to live.

Thomas Fuller operated a retail store in Cape Palmas, Liberia. He later was elected to the Liberian Senate. He wrote back to friends in Cambridge that in Liberia he had the right "not only to say what laws I will be governed by, but the privilege of aiding in making those laws."[388]

Luke Walker, a sawyer from Caroline County, emigrated with his wife and family. He found Liberia lacking in opportunities and shortages of material goods, so he and his family returned to Maryland.[389] Eben Parker emigrated from Queen Anne's County with his wife and five daughters. He

was killed by members of the Grebo tribe who thought Eben was going to raise rice and compete for their markets.[390] Stephen Allen Benson emigrated as a child with his parents from Cambridge. In 1856, he was elected Liberia's second president.[391]

Colonization was believed to be a blessing—for blacks as well as whites. Blacks would be able to live in a society free from white prejudice, and whites would be free of blacks. But in the end, few free blacks found immigration to Liberia appealing. The colonization idea failed, primarily because free blacks, most of whom had been born in the United States, simply did not want to live in Africa.[392]

Stephen Allen Benson (1816–1865), second president of Liberia. *Courtesy of the Library of Congress.*

SLAVERY'S "TRAIL OF TEARS"

While colonization did not solve the problem of what to do with the growing free black caste, the problem of the growing slave population in the Upper South did have a solution. That solution was the internal slave trade. During the fifty years before the Civil War, a million slaves from Maryland, Virginia and Kentucky were forcibly resettled to the Deep South—to Mississippi, Alabama, Louisiana and Texas—where slave labor was being sought for the cotton fields and sugar plantations.[393] This forced resettlement is slavery's "Trail of Tears."[394]

By 1800, the depletion of tobacco soil and the rise of grain agriculture and timber harvesting had transformed the work patterns on the Eastern Shore and altered the nature of slavery there. Tobacco production required a year-round labor force, but grain agriculture did not. While timber cutting could be done throughout the year, it required a predominantly male labor force. To some extent, free black labor became a more attractive economic alternative to owning slaves.[395]

Excess numbers meant that slave owners could reconfigure their labor force to improve productivity.[396] And keeping the plantation workforce at optimum level by regular slave sales could also be quite lucrative. The land records of the lower Eastern Shore counties are replete with examples.[397]

In the late summer of 1818, Thomas Freeland of Claiborne County, Mississippi, bought slaves in Talbot County. He paid Henry Catrup $525 for Philis (age twenty-six) and her six-week-old son Bill.[398] William H. Tilghman and Thomas Bullin each were paid $700 for their two slaves—eighteen-year-old Irvin Cox, "a bright mulatto," and twenty-two-year-old Jerry.[399] Joseph H. Nicholson received $2,285 for a family of six that included a thirty-eight-year-old mother, her four children (aged seven to nineteen) and a six-month-old grandson. Today, that amount of money would be worth over $36,000.[400]

At the same time that the planters of the Chesapeake found themselves with excess slaves, the United States was expanding its territory. As the country expanded, the slave system also expanded, spreading south and west across the Gulf of Mexico. Louisiana was admitted to the Union in 1812, Mississippi in 1817 and Alabama in 1819—all as slave states.[401] With this expansion of the slave system, the demand for slaves rose. And increased demand meant rising slave prices.

The trade in slaves proved to be a source of enormous profit. With lots of money to be made, new operators became involved in what was called

The sale of a slave often meant the destruction of a family. Detail from James Fuller Queen's *Journey of a Slave from the Plantation to the Battlefield. Courtesy of the Library of Congress.*

"The Business." One of the major companies in the tidewater was Franklin & Armfield, established in 1828 in nearby Alexandria. One historian called it "the largest slave-trading company in American history."[402]

Franklin & Armfield owned a large compound at 1315 Duke Street that included separate quarters for men and women slaves, a kitchen, a hospital and an outdoor area enclosed with a fence.[403] Between 1828 and 1836, about ten thousand tidewater slaves were imprisoned behind its grated iron doors. John Armfield lived above the office and handled the "collection" part of the business. His partner, Isaac Franklin, was responsible for the southern sales. The two were among the richest men in America.[404]

Franklin & Armfield employed "stringers"—agents who worked on commission, collecting slaves all around the area. Frederick Douglass described these agents. He wrote:

> *These men were generally well dressed, and very captivating in their manners; ever ready to drink, to treat, and to gamble. The fate of many a*

slave has depended upon the turn of a single card; and many a child has been snatched from the arms of its mother by bargains arranged in a state of brutal drunkenness. [405]

Some of the slaves whom Franklin & Armfield bought were sent south by ship from Alexandria and Norfolk to Charleston, Mobile and New Orleans. Most, however, were forced to walk to Louisiana and Mississippi in coffles. These trains of slaves, [406] chained together, walked fifteen to twenty miles per day for about two months in ideal conditions. [407] They walked more than one thousand miles from the Chesapeake to the slave markets of the South. Imagine walking so far. And imagine walking so far carrying pounds of iron shackles. [408]

This building was formerly the headquarters of "Franklin & Armfield, Dealers in Slaves."
Courtesy of the Library of Congress.

PLANTATIONS, SLAVERY & FREEDOM ON MARYLAND'S EASTERN SHORE

A Slave-Coffle passing the Capitol.

Courtesy of the Library of Congress.

One personal account makes this easier to visualize. Charles Ball, a Maryland slave who was bought by a slave trader, later related:

The women were merely tied together with a rope, about the size of a bed cord, which was tied like a halter round the neck of each; but the men...a strong iron collar was closely fitted by means of a padlock round each of our necks.... In addition to this, we were handcuffed in pairs, with iron staples and bolts, with a short chain, about a foot long, uniting the handcuffs and their wearers in pairs.... I could not shake off my chains, nor move a yard without the consent of my master.[409]

Coffles were typically watched over by whip- and gun-wielding men on horseback, with supply wagons bringing up the rear. Security was high. Captives were generally not allowed to talk among themselves. But, as they tramped along, sometimes they were required to sing.[410] Frederick Douglass wrote about the practice of making slaves sing: "Slaves sing most when they are most unhappy. The songs of the slave represent the sorrows of his heart; and he is relieved by them, only as an aching heart is relieved by its tears."[411]

Generally, the coffles of Franklin & Armfield walked from Alexandria, west and south across Virginia, Tennessee and Mississippi to Natchez, the Deep South's second-largest slave market. Another more northerly route included the

Routes used in the internal slave trade. *Courtesy of the author.*

paved National (or Cumberland) Road. By 1818, that road reached the Ohio River port of Wheeling, Virginia. From Wheeling, captives could be shipped by riverboat down to the Mississippi River and on to Natchez or farther on to New Orleans.[412] Other slave traders sailed from Baltimore or Norfolk, down the Atlantic coast and around Florida to Mobile or New Orleans.[413]

The nation's largest slave market was in New Orleans. Upon arrival at the slave market, the captives were washed, groomed and fed. Their skin was oiled to hide blemishes, and sometimes their hair was colored to hide their age. On sale day, they were dressed in new clothes. Then, they were subjected to minute examination from prospective buyers. Backs, especially, were checked for signs of the lash—evidence of a troublemaker.[414]

From 1831 to 1835, fifteen different slave traders advertised in the *Cambridge Chronicle* that they wished to make purchases in Dorchester County. Sometimes these were stringers working for outside firms, promising to "pay the highest cash price." Others were Eastern Shore firms such as John N. Denning & Co., Woolfolks, C.S. & J.M. Knight and Overly & Sanders. These four firms had regular agents in Cambridge.

John N. Denning & Co.'s headquarters was in Centreville in Queen Anne's County. The company had a slave pen there for its own use, and it also rented space (for twenty-five cents per day) to slave owners who needed a place to keep slaves they were preparing to sell. Denning & Co. advertised

NEGROES WANTED,

We at all times wish to purchase any number of negroes, of both sexes; either slaves for life or a term of years, that are sound and healthy, and good titles, for which we will pay more money in gold than any other Maryland traders. We are permanently located at this place, where we have fitted up a place for the safe keeping of negroes, at 25 cents per day. Persons having servants to dispose of, will do well to see us, as we are at all times buying and forwarding to the different Southern markets, and will always pay the highest prices the Southern markets will justify. All communications, (post-paid, and not otherwise,) will be promptly attended to, if addressed to
JOHN N. DENNING & CO.
Centreville, Queen Ann's county,
May 27, 1843.   1y   Maryland.

From the *Kent News*, May 27, 1843.

Kent News, Chestertown, Maryland.

that it was buying both "slaves for life" and slaves with "a term of years" to serve. It is doubtful, however, that those terms were abided by once the slaves were sold to Georgia, Mississippi, Louisiana or Texas.[415]

One of the most notorious trading companies on the Eastern Shore was Woolfolks.[416] Austin Woolfolk first worked with his father in Augusta, Georgia, selling Georgia slaves to supply the new plantations in Alabama. He came north after the War of 1812 to look for a larger quantity of slaves than he was able to buy in the South.[417]

His first advertisements on the Eastern Shore began to appear in 1816. Easton began an annual slave auction in 1818, but rather than buy his slaves there, Austin Woolfolk cut out the middleman by going directly to the slave owners. Soon Woolfolks was known by reputation everywhere on the Eastern Shore. Woolfolks agents set up temporary headquarters at local inns or taverns, distributed handbills and took out newspaper advertisements. It eventually established its headquarters in Easton, and Joseph Woolfolk, Austin's brother, came to Maryland to run that business.

Slaves whom Woolfolks purchased were shipped to Baltimore, where they were held in the Woolfolks jail on Pratt Street (at Fremont, not far from present-day Oriole Park at Camden Yards).[418] When a full shipment had been collected, the slaves were shipped from Fells Point down the Atlantic coast and around the Florida peninsula to New Orleans.

By the 1820s, Woolfolks was shipping between 250 and 450 slaves from Maryland annually, many in surplus privateers left over from the War of 1812. Between 1819 and 1831, over 4,304 slaves are documented as having been sent by the ocean-going trade from Baltimore to New Orleans. Woolfolks accounted for 53 percent of them.[419]

Cash for Negroes.

THE Subscriber wishes to purchase one hundred likely young slaves, from the age, of 12 to 25 years: for which he will pay the highest cash prices. Persons disposed to sell will please call on him at Mr. Lowe's Tavern, in Easton, where he can be found at all times.
June 21.   J. B. WOOLFOLK.

From the *Cambridge Chronicle*, June 21, 1816.

SLAVES SHIPPED FROM BALTIMORE
1819-31

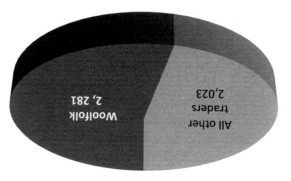

All other traders 2,023

Woolfolk 2,281

Graph 5. Slaves Shipped from Baltimore, 1819–1831.

MARYLAND'S OWN *AMISTAD*

Not all slaves went south "quietly."

Most people know the story of the *Amistad*, the slave ship that was shanghaied by its victims in 1839 and recaptured. Following a famous Supreme Court case in which John Quincy Adams defended the victims, all were released.

Thirteen years before the *Amistad* adventure, Austin Woolfolk lost some of his slaves in a similar manner.[420] In late April 1826, a group of thirty-one slaves was walked in chains from Woolfolk's pen, down Pratt Street to a Fells Point wharf. There the slaves were put in small boats and rowed out to the schooner *Decatur*, which was captained by Walter Galloway.

Galloway had been captaining his slaver for years. His practice was that, once out at sea, he allowed small groups of slaves to be brought above deck. On this particular voyage, five days out, two slaves pushed Captain Galloway overboard. When crewman William Porter heard the splash and went to investigate, Porter likewise was pushed overboard.

By mid-morning, the slaves were in possession of the ship, but they did not know how to sail it. The ship drifted off the Eastern Seaboard for almost a week before it was stopped and recaptured by a whaling ship. The whalers took about half the slaves aboard their own ship. They left the schooner's crew and fourteen male slaves on the *Decatur*. Three days later, a brig took those slaves to New York, where all of them escaped into the city.

We know about this incident because one of the slaves who escaped was later captured in West Chester, New York, tried for the murder of Captain Galloway and crewman Porter and executed. The trial was reported in a Baltimore newspaper. The editor of the paper, Benjamin Lundy, called Austin Woolfolk "a monster in human shape." Then, one day in 1827, Woolfolk attacked Lundy on the street. He threw Lundy to the ground, beat him severely and then walked away.[421]

Woolfolk was tried on the charge of attempted murder and found guilty. His punishment was a fine of one dollar. Judge Nicholas Brice praised the slave trade's economic benefit to Maryland and said Woolfolks had removed "a great many rogues and vagabonds who are a nuisance in the state."[422]

THE PANIC OF 1837

In 1837, questionable lending practices, inflated paper money and speculation in western public lands led to a financial crisis that brought on a major recession. Prices for farm goods plummeted. Marginal slaveholders in the Upper South saw selling their slaves as a way to get out of debt.[423] Some of those planters lived on Hoopers Island.

According to the 1840 Census, Hoopers Island was a community of 463 people. Both the white population and the free black population had grown slightly during the previous decade. But the number of slaves on the island had fallen rather dramatically—from 69 slaves in 1830 to 43 slaves in 1840.[424] That is a 37.5 percent drop and more than twice the percentage drop that one finds in Dorchester County as a whole.[425]

These sales affected whole communities and often tore slave families apart. Some of the slaves who were sold were third- or fourth-generation residents on the same plantation.[426] To assuage the conscience of some of the white owners, Eastern Shore slave traders often included in their advertisements a promise not to separate families.[427] But that promise meant little. Slave sales broke up one slave marriage in five and separated one-third of children under fourteen from one or both of their parents.[428]

RUNNING AWAY

$300 REWARD,

Will be given for the apprehension of negro woman

NELLY KEENE,

and her seven or eight children

if taken out of this state—$200 if taken in the state and out of the county—or if in the county, one hundred dollars will be given—provided they shall be secured so that the subscriber gets them again: Or a proportionate reward will be paid for the delivery of any of them. They ranaway on Wednesday night, the 6th inst & are no doubt all together and accompanied by her husband and their father, Joe Keene, by whom they were decoyed. They embarked in a sail-canoe, belonging also to the subscriber, about 23 feet long, white above the water, with one gaff-sail, it having been stript of the other sails, & being pioneered by Joe, who is a sailor of some experience and notoriety, and a shrewd, crafty fellow now a fugitive from a southern master, they will unquestionably make good use of their time, and probably aim to pass up the bay and through the C. & D. Can–l. Joe is about 50 years old and five feet 4 or 5 inches high.

NELLY aforesaid, his wife is about 35 years old, 5 feet 1 or two 2 inches high, of chesnut color and pregnant.

ELIZA is about 18 years old, 4 feet 8 or 9 inches high, well made, likely and of a light chesnut color.

JOE 17 years of age, about 5 feet high, is also well made and of a chesnut color.

GEORGE is about 16, 4 feet 8 or 10 inches high.

It is deemed unnecessary to describe the smaller negroes, as they are in all probability in company with the larger ones.

LEVIN WOOLFORD.

Parson's Creek, Dor. Co. Md. April 9.

From the *Easton Gazette*, April 13, 1831.

With horrible tales about conditions in the Deep South and stringers buying up local slaves, it is not surprising that more and more Eastern Shore slaves were running away. By this time, the price of slaves was so high that few could save enough money to buy their way out of slavery. Many more could flee.[429]

On the Eastern Shore, geography was a factor. Maryland was situated just south of the free state of Pennsylvania; equally important, the rivers of the Eastern Shore helped runaways. In the nineteenth century, the Choptank, from its mouth at the Chesapeake, was navigable for nearly forty miles upstream, almost to the Delaware line. The Nanticoke was navigable from the bay all the way to Seaford, Delaware.[430] And of course, Baltimore was a short sail across the Chesapeake.

Advertisements offering rewards for the apprehension of runaways often included references to local waterways. When Nelly Keene "and her seven or eight children" ran away from Levin Woolford of Parsons Creek in Dorchester County, his advertisement noted:

They embarked in a sail-canoe, belonging also to the subscriber, about 23-feet long, white above the water, with one gaff-sail, it having been stripped of the other sails, & being pioneered by Joe, who is a sailor of some experience and notoriety and a shrewd, crafty fellow—now a fugitive from a southern master. They will unquestionably make good use of their time and probably aim to pass up the Bay and through the C&D Canal.[431]

Similarly, when Bob, Jake and George, three slaves belonging to John Simmons and Jacob Pattison, ran away from Taylor's Island, the fugitives stole a large bateau (or skipjack) named the *Fox of Parsons Creek* from a neighboring farmer in order to make their getaway. The boat was found near Baltimore, so the owners presumed that their slaves were "lurking about the city, or may probably attempt to make their way to Pennsylvania."[432]

400 DOLLARS REWARD.—Ranaway from the subscribers living on Taylor's Island, Dorchester County, Maryland, on Saturday October 1st. a negro man named BOB, aged about 23 years, of a dark chesnut color, and 5 feet 6 or 7 inches high. He had on when he went away a pair of blue pantaloons and cloth coat, his other clothing not recollected. He took with him a large Batteau named "Fox of Parson's Creek" belonging to Mr. J. M. Pattison—which Batteau has been found at the Spring Gardens near this city. Also a Negro Man named JAKE, about the same height as Bob, is very black, clothing &c. not recollected. Also a Negro Boy named GEORGE, about 17 or 18 years of age, about 5 feet high, near of same colour as Bob, clothing not recollected. We will give $150 Reward for either Bob or Jake, if taken in the State, or $300 for either if taken out of the State, and $100 for George if taken either in or out of the State, provided in either case they be delivered to the subscribers or secured in any jail so that we get them again.

From the circumstance of the batteau being found in this city, it is presumed they are lurking about the city, or may probably attempt to make their way to Pennsylvania. JOHN SIMMONS,
oc 15   d&tentf   JACOB PATTISON.

$300 REWARD.—Ranaway from the subscriber on Sunday night, the 26th inst. three Negroes, to wit: LEWIS, supposed to be about twenty five years old, five feet ten inches high, of a black complexion, has a very bad countenance. face rather sharp, with thick lips. He was purchased a few years since of Maj. Richard Jones of the city of Annapolis.

JOHN DRAKE—Is about twenty-one or two years old—say five feet nine inches high, is a likely looking, stout made fellow, of a bright complexion, talks with his mouth partly shut, and has a pleasant countenance.

EMORY DRAKE—He is brother to John, very much of his complexion and features, talks like him with his mouth also partly shut—is, say five feet high, and about sixteen years of age. It is not known that said negroes took any clothing with them, except what they had on, which was a shirt, drab cloth jacket and linen trowsers.

John and Emory's mother is a free mulatto woman by the name of Hannah, and resides in Baltimore, where it is supposed they may have gone. Having taken a sail boat of Mr. Thomas J. Sherwood's of the adjoining farm. She is twenty feet long, painted black with a yellow stripe three or four inches wide, dividing the black. The above reward will be given if taken out of the State, but one hundred and fifty dollars if taken in the State, and lodged in jail in the city of Baltimore or Easton, Md. so that I get them again.   EDWARD P. GOLLORTHON.

Talbott County, near St. Michaels.   jy 2
☞The Republican, Annapolis; Cecil Whig, Elkton; Delaware Journal, Wilmington, Del. will publish the above to amount of $2 each and charge this office.   2aw1t

From the *American & Commercial Daily Advertiser,* (*above*) October 15, 1836; (*right*) July 2, 1842.

John Simmons and Jacob Pattison knew that many slaves on the Eastern Shore were encouraged to run away by the ease with which they could blend into the collection of blacks (slave and free) who made up the population of Baltimore. Edward Gollorthon, who lived in Talbot County near St. Michaels, also understood that situation. When his three slaves—Lewis, and John and Emory Drake—ran away, Gollorthon wrote in his July 2, 1842 advertisement that he believed the three were heading for Baltimore.[433] (These three slaves also had stolen a sailboat.) John and Emory Drake's mother was a free mulatto woman by the name of Hannah who lived in the city. The growth in the free black population after the Revolutionary War, especially in urban areas, meant that blacks were now numerous enough to hide large numbers of runaways.[434] John and Emory's owner knew that Hannah could help the three slaves "disappear."

Gollorthon advertised that he would pay a reward if these slaves were apprehended and "lodged in jail" in Baltimore or in Easton. Slave owners considered the public jail to be an extension of their plantations. In a 2016 op-ed article in the *Baltimore Sun*, two Towson University graduate students noted that in the nineteenth century, "slave owners traveling through Baltimore checked their slaves into a jail, while the owners slept comfortably in a nearby inn."[435]

FRED "FREDDIE" BAILEY—THE SLAVE

In February 1818, a young slave named Freddie Bailey was born in northeastern Talbot County, near Hillsborough on Tuckahoe Creek. His slave mother was black; his father was white. It was rumored that his father was his owner, Aaron Anthony.

Aaron Anthony owned two or three farms of his own and about thirty slaves, but his properties were managed by an overseer. Meanwhile, Captain Anthony was the general overseer for Edward Lloyd, who was probably the wealthiest man on the Eastern Shore. Anthony managed Lloyd's thirteen farms and hundreds of slaves. Captain Anthony was essentially "the overseer of overseers."[436] He lived on the great Wye River Plantation, which had been in the Lloyd family since 1659.[437] The first Wye House, started in 1770, was destroyed by the British in the American Revolution. The house was rebuilt in 1784.

Edward Lloyd is a name you have read before in these chapters. This Edward Lloyd was the fifth in his family of that name. He was descended from seventeenth-century Maryland "old money." When his father died in 1796, this Edward Lloyd had inherited 12,360 acres of land in Talbot, Queen Anne's and Caroline Counties; 320 slaves; and a 2,500-volume library.[438]

Edward Lloyd was a congressman, governor of Maryland from 1809 to 1811 and a U.S. senator from 1819 to 1826. He also was a colonel in the Maryland militia. Francis Scott Key married his sister Mary. But today, this Edward Lloyd's biggest claim to fame probably is that Freddie Bailey (whom the world knows as Frederick Douglass) once lived on his Wye River Plantation.

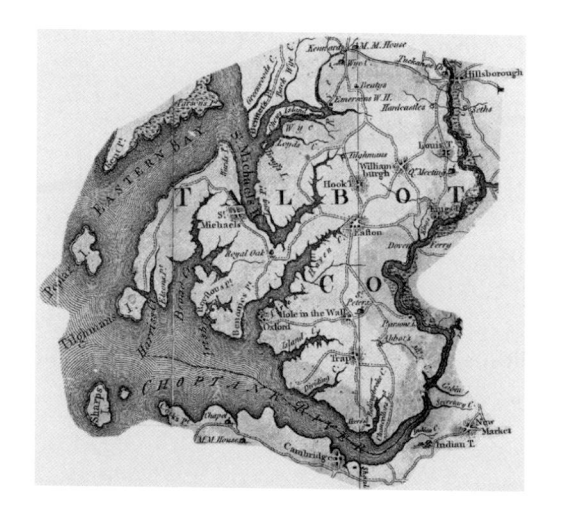

Talbot County, 1795. *Courtesy of Freepages.rootsweb.*

Freddie Bailey was raised by his grandmother. When he was about six years old, he was taken to "the big house," the Wye Plantation, twelve miles away. There, he often was mistreated by a slave called Aunt Katy who ran both the kitchen and the children.[439] The little boy was befriended by Lucretia Anthony Auld, the twenty-year-old daughter of his owner Aaron Anthony. Lucretia may have been Freddie's half sister.[440]

Years later, Frederick Douglass remembered his time at Wye River Plantation. In his 1855 autobiography, he wrote:

> *Colonel Lloyd could not brook any contradiction from a slave. When he spoke, a slave must stand, listen, and tremble; and such was literally the case. I have seen Colonel Lloyd make old Barney, a man between fifty and sixty years of age, uncover his bald head, kneel down upon the cold, damp ground, and receive upon his naked and toil-worn shoulders more than thirty lashes at the time.*[441]

When Freddie Bailey was about eight years old, he was sent to Baltimore to live with Lucretia Anthony Auld's brother-in-law Hugh Auld, who was a ship's carpenter. The Aulds lived in Fells Point at 1815 Aliceanna Street (near today's Broadway Market). Freddie's job was to look after the Aulds' little boy Thomas. It was a much better situation than what Freddie had experienced at Wye Plantation. On the Eastern Shore, Aunt Katy had treated him like a pig; in Baltimore, the Aulds treated him like a child. He had enough food to eat and sufficient clothing. He even had time to play in the street like the young boy that he was. Frederick Douglass later said that this removal from the Lloyd plantation was "one of the most interesting and fortunate events of my life."[442]

Hugh Auld's wife, Sophia, was a weaver who had never before owned a slave. She taught Freddie the alphabet, until her husband put a stop to the lessons, telling his wife that such teaching was unlawful. And besides, learning would make a slave unmanageable and therefore of no value to his master. Frederick Douglass later said that at that moment he understood what gave the white man power to enslave the black man, and from then on, he was determined to learn. He made friends with all the white boys he met in the street, and they became his teachers.[443]

When Aaron Anthony died in 1826 and his assets were divided among his heirs, Freddie Bailey became the property of Lucretia Anthony Auld and her husband, Thomas. By this time, Hugh Auld had moved the family to Philpot Street near the wharves, where he and a friend had opened their own shipyard, Auld & Harrison, Shipbuilders. Fred Bailey went to work at the shipyard doing odd jobs.

He also acquired a popular schoolbook titled *The Columbian Orator*—a collection of essays, poems and dialogues that was used to teach reading and eloquence. Fred practiced his new skill by reading speeches by great orators like Socrates, Cicero, Sheridan and William Pitt.[444]

Fred Bailey learned to write by copying the letters marked on the lumber in the shipyards. *S* meant starboard, and *L* meant larboard. (Today, we usually say port.) *F* equaled forward, or fore, and *A*, aft. He decided that if he could make these four letters, he could make more. He practiced by copying the letters in young Thomas Auld's discarded copy books.[445]

THE LASH.

Detail from James Fuller Queen's *Journey of a Slave from the Plantation to the Battlefield. Courtesy of the Library of Congress.*

When he was about fifteen years old, Fred Bailey was returned to his Eastern Shore owner. Hugh Auld's shipbuilding business had failed, and he and his brother had had a falling out.[446] By this time, Thomas Auld, who had been a sea captain, was a merchant in St. Michaels. Lucretia Auld had died, and Thomas had remarried. Fred Bailey was treated much harsher in St. Michaels than in Baltimore, and for the first time in seven years, he was hungry.[447]

In 1833, Thomas Auld sent Fred Bailey to work for Edward Covey, a poor farmer who regularly beat his slaves to "break" them.[448] Now, for the first time in his life, Fred Bailey was a field hand. And for the first six months, he was whipped every week.[449]

Covey's weapon of choice was a cowskin. Frederick Douglass described this "terrible instrument":

A "cowskin" is a kind of whip seldom seen in the northern states. It is made entirely of untanned, but dried, ox hide, and is about as hard as a piece of well-seasoned live oak. It is made of various sizes, but the usual length is about three feet. The part held in the hand is nearly an inch in thickness; and, from the extreme end of the butt or handle, the cowskin tapers its whole length to a point. This makes it quite elastic and springy. A blow with it, on the hardest back, will gash the flesh.... [It is] worse than a cat-o-nine tails. It condenses the whole strength of the arm to a single point, and comes with a spring that makes the air whistle.[450]

Covey's beatings were brutal. Douglass later wrote, "Under his [Covey's] heavy blows, blood flowed freely, and wales were left on my back as large as my little finger. The sores on my back, from this flogging, continued for weeks, for they were kept open by the rough and coarse cloth which I wore for shirting."[451] At age sixteen, Fred Bailey was so severely beaten that he was "broken in body, soul, and spirit."[452]

In 1836, Fred Bailey plotted with five friends to run away. But before they could even begin their escape, their owners got wind of the venture (probably one of the group betrayed them). They were locked up in the Talbot County jail in Easton. Fred Bailey knew the danger that he faced by this attempt to escape. When he had lived in Baltimore, he had heard coffles of slaves being moved through Philpot Street in the early morning hours to the ships that would take them south. Later, he wrote:

If a slave was convicted of any high misdemeanor, became unmanageable, or evinced a determination to run away, he was...severely whipped, put on board the sloop, carried to Baltimore, and sold to Austin Woolfolk, or some other slave trader, as a warning to the slaves remaining.[453]

Surprisingly, instead of selling him south, Thomas Auld sent Fred Bailey back to his brother in Baltimore, with the promise that if Fred learned a trade and behaved he would be freed at age twenty-five. (That would not be for seven more years.) Fred trained as a caulker, a skilled job in the shipyard, for which he was paid a dollar and a half a day—money which he had to give to Hugh Auld.[454]

Fred also joined the East Baltimore Mental Improvement Society. There he met and fell in love with Anna Murray, a free black from Caroline County. The two planned how he would escape from slavery. Anna sold her feather bed to get money. Fred borrowed seaman's protection papers from a retired free black sailor. These were papers that American sailors had used in foreign ports since 1796 as proof of their citizenship. With their embossed American eagle at the top, the papers looked very official.

FREDERICK DOUGLASS—FUGITIVE

On September 3, 1838, Fred Bailey, dressed as a sailor, boarded the new Philadelphia, Wilmington and Baltimore Railroad heading north. The conductor did not question his sailor's papers. In Wilmington, he took the steamboat for Philadelphia, where he boarded a second train for New York. His escape had taken less than twenty-four hours.[455]

In New York, a sailor he met on the wharves connected him with David Ruggles of the New York Vigilance Committee, an abolitionist group that helped fugitive slaves. Anna joined Fred in New York, and they were married. The couple then moved to New Bedford, Massachusetts, where Ruggles thought Fred might find work as a caulker. It was a free black there named Nathan Johnson who gave Fred Bailey the name of Frederick Douglass—taking it from the name of a Scottish lord in Sir Walter Scott's poem *The Lady of the Lake*.[456]

As it happened, in New Bedford, Frederick Douglass could get only unskilled jobs. White caulkers in the shipyards threatened to walk off the job if he was hired as a caulker.[457] Prejudice knows no geographical bounds. Douglass had escaped from the chattel slavery of Maryland to the caste slavery of Massachusetts. Of course, legally, Frederick Douglass was still a slave. And now, he was a fugitive. We will revisit this Eastern Shore runaway in our final chapter.

IN SUMMARY

In this chapter, we have seen that in the late eighteenth and early nineteenth centuries, the free black population of the Eastern Shore exploded. But as the numbers of free blacks increased, their rights were steadily taken away. Racial prejudice on the Eastern Shore led to the creation of an inflexible two-caste system. Free blacks were encouraged to immigrate to the State of Maryland in Liberia. Few went. Instead, they became African Americans and developed their own institutions and culture.

After the American Revolution, the indigenous slave population grew as well. But as economic conditions on the Eastern Shore changed, farmers needed fewer slaves and now had excess labor. Hundreds of Eastern Shore slaves were sold to slave traders. As more slaves were "sold South," the number of runaways increased—among them Fred Bailey. He fled to New England, took the new name of Frederick Douglass and experienced racial prejudice "Northern style."

4

ABOLITION, THE FUGITIVE SLAVE ACT AND THE UNDERGROUND RAILROAD

I n this fourth chapter, as in the first, we are going to put the happenings on Maryland's Eastern Shore into a bigger context by looking at the abolition movement, the Fugitive Slave Act and the Underground Railroad. First, a look at abolition.

ABOLITION

Ideas about abolishing slavery go back a long way in American history.[458] The popularity of the idea ebbed and flowed. After the Revolutionary War, just as many people favored manumission, some people thought the time was right to completely phase out slavery.

In November 1789, Nicholas Hammond, a slave-owning delegate from Dorchester County, introduced a bill in the Maryland Senate—"An Act to Promote the gradual abolition of Slavery and to prevent the rigorous Exportation of Negros and Mulattos from this State."[459] The Senate, realizing "the great importance of this subject," proposed to form a joint committee with the House of Delegates to work on the bill. But many members of the Lower House had a strong aversion to abolition. So, by a vote of thirty-nine to fifteen, the House of Delegates refused to cooperate with the Senate, effectively tabling the bill, in order, they said, "to avoid the temper and Irritation" that discussion of such a bill would cause.[460]

On the Eastern Shore, there were public meetings in Queen Anne's, Kent, Talbot, Dorchester, Caroline and Worcester Counties in which citizens called upon the General Assembly to act on ending slavery.[461] In 1790, the Choptank Abolition Society was formed in Caroline County and the Chester River Abolition Society in Chestertown. These groups petitioned Congress to end the African slave trade and to make it illegal for foreign ships to be refitted for the slave trade in U.S. shipyards. The Eastern Shore abolition societies also hired lawyers to help local blacks with their freedom suits. In that endeavor, they were quite successful.[462]

In 1789 in Baltimore, the Quaker philanthropist Elisha Tyson, who owned Woodbury Mill on the Jones Falls, helped organize a group that called itself by the long name of the Maryland Society for Promoting the Abolition of Slavery and the Relief of Poor Negroes and Others Unlawfully Held in Bondage. The group soon had more than two hundred members.[463]

While there are these examples, in general the idea of abolition got little traction in eighteenth-century Maryland. And in 1791, the House of Delegates came within two votes of declaring the Baltimore abolition society "subversive to the rights of our citizens."[464] The Maryland legislature then went on to make it even more difficult for slaves to win the freedom suits that abolitionists supported. The Maryland abolition movement never recovered from the new repressive legislation, and by the late 1790s, the Baltimore abolition group was essentially dismantled.[465]

Any real hope of abolishing slavery in the United States disappeared when Eli Whitney invented the cotton gin in 1793. His machine could remove seeds from the cotton boll much faster than humans, so the demand for picked cotton rose dramatically. And if you needed more cotton bolls to feed the gin, you needed more labor in the fields picking cotton.

Cotton exports skyrocketed after the gin was invented. In 1790, the United States exported 1,601,000 pounds of cotton; in 1800, 17,790,000; and, in 1820, 35,000,000 pounds.[466]

Of course, a market for all that cotton was also required. The textile mills of Lancashire in Britain, once they were powered by Watt's steam engine, could handle all the cotton that the South could produce.[467] Their demand for cotton essentially kept the American plantation in business. By 1860, Britain was using ten times more cotton than in 1800, and American planters had become among "the richest and most influential people in the world."[468]

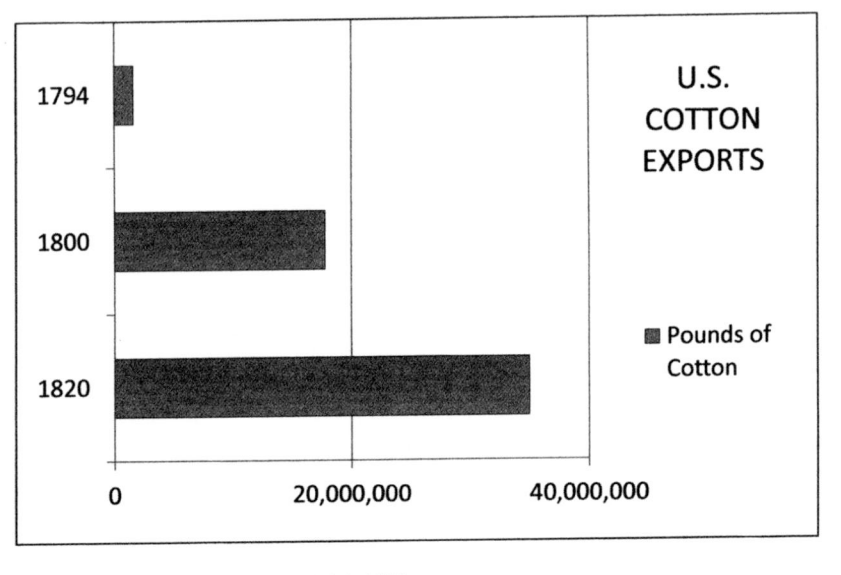

GRAPH 6. U.S. COTTON EXPORTS, 1794–1820.

THE POWER OF THE PRESS

In the 1820s and '30s, abolition became a bigger movement in the United States. White abolitionists tended to focus on how slavery distorted democracy and corrupted Christianity, how it damaged the work ethic and twisted basic human relations.[469] Black abolitionists, on the other hand, emphasized the slaves' suffering, the physical and psychological abuse they endured and the multiple ways in which slavery denied men and women a normal life.[470] Slave owners, of course, combated both groups of abolitionists with the picture of the happy slave whose dependency reflected his inferiority and justified the role of the white master.

Newspapers played a big role in spreading abolitionist ideas, and Maryland had its own abolitionist newspaper. The *Genius of Universal Emancipation* was established in Baltimore in 1824 by Benjamin Lundy.[471] (As mentioned in the previous chapter, Lundy was attacked on the streets of Baltimore by the slave trader Austin Woolfolk.)

In 1829, Lundy hired William Lloyd Garrison from Newburyport, Massachusetts, to be the editor of his paper. It did not take long for Garrison to attract attention. Garrison wrote in one of his columns that Francis Todd,

101

a ship captain from his own hometown of Newburyport, was a highway robber and a murderer. Todd had used his boat to take a large number of slaves (eighty or more) from a plantation in Anne Arundel County to New Orleans. Garrison wrote that for this act Todd should be sentenced to solitary confinement for life.[472]

After Captain Todd read Garrison's article, he sued. Garrison was convicted of libel and fined fifty dollars. When he refused to pay the fine, he was put in prison. He served forty-four days until a sympathizer paid the money that he owed.

Freddie Bailey was living in Baltimore at that time. He said that the word *abolition* was always used in connections that made it an interesting word to him. He later wrote: "If a slave ran away and succeeded in getting clear, or if a slave killed his master, set fire to a barn, or did anything very wrong in the mind of a slaveholder, it was spoken of as the fruit of *abolition*."[473]

After William Lloyd Garrison was freed from jail, he returned to New England, where he became famous for his own abolitionist newspaper, *The Liberator*. In it, he began to write in support of complete and immediate emancipation.[474] He had seen the internal slave trade up close in

Both images courtesy of the Library of Congress.

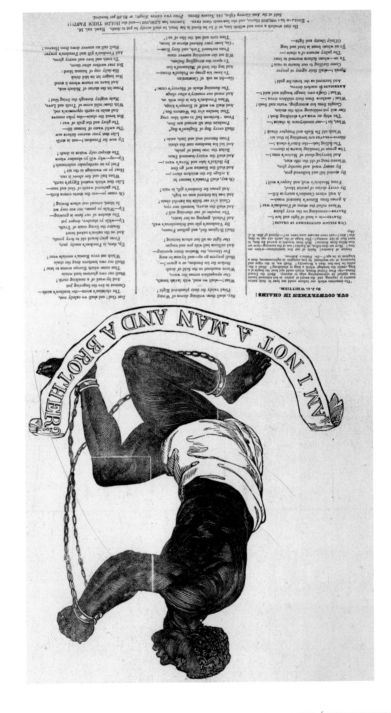

Abolitionist broadside, 1837. *Courtesy of the Library of Congress.*

Maryland. In the October 5, 1833 edition of *The Liberator*, he wrote: "I do believe that Virginia is become another Guinea, and the Eastern Shore an African coast."[475]

The same year that Garrison wrote that statement (1833), the British abolished slavery as a part of the Whig Party's massive Reform movement. Their abolition act specified that Negroes born after January 1, 1834, would be free. For people already enslaved, the law set up an apprenticeship stage of seven years. When slaves became free, owners were compensated.[476]

Nationally, abolition was becoming a stronger movement. In the 1830s, John Greenleaf Whittier's antislavery poem "Our Countrymen in Chains" was reproduced on broadsides and widely distributed throughout the northern states. This poem and other similar ones written by Whittier were strong condemnations of slavery and of those who supported it.[477] In addition to the Whittier poem, the broadside included two further statements that were meant to make a moral appeal to end slavery: "He that stealeth a man and selleth him, or if he be found in his hand, he shall surely be put to death." (Exodus 21:16) and "England has 800,000 slaves, and she has made them free. America has 2,250,000! And she holds them fast!!!!"

FREDERICK DOUGLASS—ABOLITIONIST

By this point, Frederick Douglass, fugitive slave from Maryland, was living in New Bedford, Massachusetts. There, for four years, he sawed wood, rolled oil casks, swept chimneys, shoveled coal—whatever menial labor he was allowed to do.[478] Meanwhile, he began attending antislavery meetings and subscribing to abolitionist newspapers. In 1841, Douglass attended a large antislavery convention in Nantucket.

A prominent Massachusetts abolitionist named William C. Coffin had heard Douglass speak to a group of blacks in New Bedford. Coffin asked Douglass to describe his experiences as a slave to the Nantucket convention.[479] After his talk, the leaders of the Massachusetts Anti-Slavery Society asked him to become one of their agents. Thus began Frederick Douglass's work as an abolitionist orator. When Douglass was introduced in the Anti-Slavery Society gatherings, he was usually described as a "graduate from 'the peculiar institution,' with his diploma written on his back."[480]

It was unusual to find a fugitive slave lecturer, and sometimes large groups assembled to hear him speak. To prevent his owner Thomas Auld from

Frontispiece of *Narrative of the Life of Frederick Douglass, an American Slave*, 1845.

finding him, Frederick Douglass never told his former name, his owner's name or the state or county where he came from. Eventually, people began to doubt that Douglass had ever been a slave, and he was denounced as an imposter. Later, he wrote: "They said I did not talk like a slave, look like a slave, nor act like a slave, and that they believed I had never been south of Mason and Dixon's line."[481]

To dispel all the doubt, he wrote the story of his life—naming names, places and dates. *Narrative of the Life of Frederick Douglass, an American Slave* was published in 1845, seven years after his escape from Maryland.

The publication of Douglass's autobiography, of course, exposed him to recapture. He had committed a double crime. He had run away, and now he had exposed all the "dirty little secrets" of slavery on the Eastern Shore and in Baltimore. So, with his friends' support, he fled to Europe.[482]

In 1846, two English Friends, Anna and Ellen Richardson, bought Frederick Douglass's freedom. First, Thomas Auld sold twenty-eight-year-old Frederick Bailey to his brother Hugh Auld.[483] Then, the Richardson sisters paid Hugh Auld £150 sterling for Douglass's freedom. Papers were filed in Baltimore in December 1846.[484] Douglass could now return to the United States.

In 1848, Frederick Douglass moved to Rochester, New York, where he published *The North Star* newspaper. He and his wife, Anna, also helped slaves escape across Lake Ontario to St. Catharines, Canada, as part of the Underground Railroad. Slavery had been abolished in Canada in the late eighteenth century (thirty years before it was abolished in England). After the War of 1812, Canada openly welcomed runaways. In Canada, former slaves were granted land, citizenship and the right to vote.[485]

THE EXPANSION OF SLAVERY QUESTION

In time, Frederick Douglass became a leader of the abolition movement. His writings and eloquent speeches sharply refuted the belief of many slaveholders that blacks were mentally inferior. But Douglass's words did nothing to convince those in power in the slave states that human bondage should be ended. Rather, those men continually sought to expand slavery.

In the nineteenth century, as the population of the United States both grew and expanded westward, the big questions of the day were: What sort of society ultimately would shape the West? Should we allow slavery to expand into the western territories? Constitutionally, does Congress have the power to restrict slavery when it admits new states into the Union?[486]

The expansion of slavery issue first was debated in 1820 when Missouri applied for admission to the Union.[487] Many settlers who moved into the Missouri Territory had come from the cotton states, bringing their slaves with them. Naturally, they wanted Missouri to be a slave state. But, many northerners did not want to see slavery extended beyond the Mississippi River.

The 1820 controversy was settled by compromise. Missouri was admitted to the Union without restriction as to slavery, but all remaining portions of the Louisiana Purchase north of the 36° 30' latitude line were to be forever free.

In the 1830s and '40s, the issue of expanding slavery again was debated in conjunction with Texas. When Texas declared its independence from

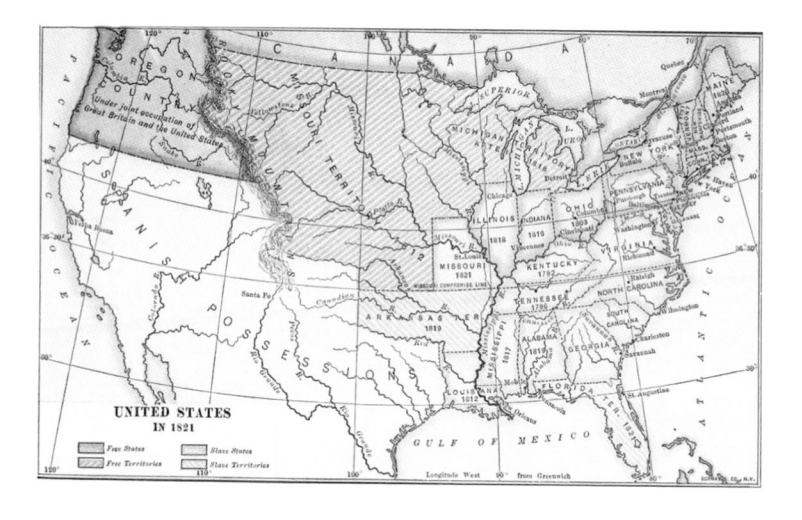

United States Territorial Growth, 1821. *Courtesy of Wikimedia Commons.*

Mexico in 1835, the United States quickly recognized the independent republic. Then a push began for Texas to join the Union. Southern states supported the idea of gaining new slave territory. Northern states protested the annexation.

Since the Missouri Compromise, Congress had been flooded with thousands of antislavery petitions. Many of them were introduced by former president John Quincy Adams, who had been elected to Congress from Massachusetts in 1830. Adams was not an abolitionist, but he was an ardent supporter of the citizen's right to petition the government. In 1836, Congress passed a "gag rule" that prohibited the introduction of antislavery petitions. Adams got around the prohibition by labeling them petitions against Texas annexation.[488]

Congress voted to admit Texas in 1845. That annexation, boundary disputes and the expansionist policy of the United States led to war with Mexico in 1846.

ARAMINTA "MINTY" ROSS—SLAVE

On Maryland's Eastern Shore in 1849 (the year after the Mexican War ended), a slave named Harriet Tubman ran away. She was one of 279 Maryland slaves who escaped that year.[489]

Harriet had been born in March 1822 on the Anthony Thompson plantation south of Madison in Dorchester County. She was the daughter of two slaves, Harriet Green (who was called "Rit" or "Ritta") and Benjamin Ross. Originally, she was named Araminta Ross and called "Minty."[490]

While Minty's parents were both slaves, Harriet Green and Ben Ross had different masters. Because of that, Minty Ross's story is intertwined with the stories of a number of white families in the area where she lived. Minty Ross's mother was owned by Atthow Pattison, who owned a plantation in central Dorchester County. When Pattison died in 1797, he willed to his granddaughter Mary Pattison one enslaved girl named "Rittia and her increase, until she and they arrive at forty-five years of age."[491]

In 1800, Mary Pattison married Joseph Brodess, a local farmer from Bucktown, south of Cambridge. And in June 1801, she gave birth to a son, Edward. Sometime after 1802, Joseph Brodess died, leaving Mary a young widow. About a year after her husband's death, Mary Brodess married Anthony Thompson, a widower with three young sons, who owned property near the Blackwater River.

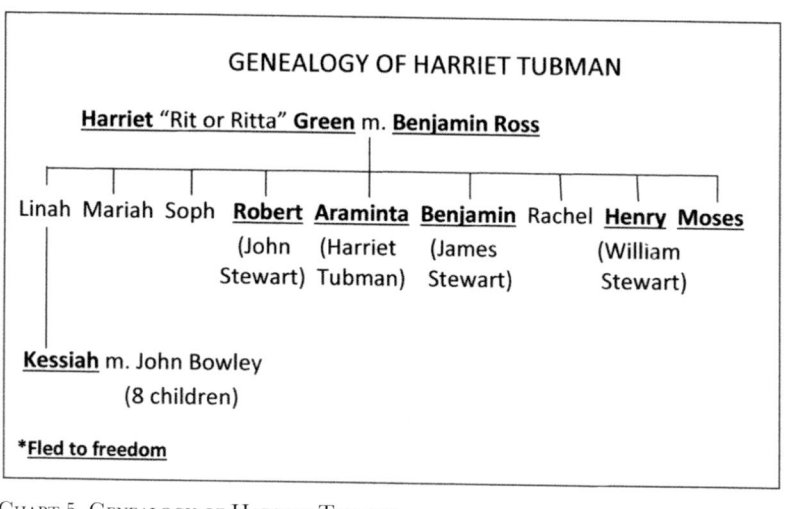

CHART 5. GENEALOGY OF HARRIET TUBMAN.

When Mary Brodess married Anthony Thompson and moved into his household, she brought her personal slave Rit Green. One of Thompson's slaves was Benjamin Ross, a highly skilled and valued timber man who managed the operations on Thompson's heavily forested property. Thus, Rit and Ben became members of the same household. Eventually, they married and, about 1808, started their own family.

Mary Thompson died about 1810, leaving Edward Brodess under the guardianship of his stepfather, Anthony Thompson. Edward was now the owner of Rit and her children.[492] In late 1823 or early 1824, Edward Brodess moved back to his own farm in Bucktown, about ten miles east of the Thompson plantation, taking Rit and her children (including Minty, who was a baby). When Brodess took his slaves to his own farm, he split up the Ross family, as Ben Ross was still a slave living on the Thompson property. (Later, Brodess permanently fractured the Ross family when he sold Rit's three eldest daughters to out-of-state buyers.) In March 1824, Edward Brodess married Eliza Ann Keene.

A SERIES OF TEMPORARY MASTERS

When Minty Ross was about six or seven years old, the little girl was put to work. As had been the case with Freddie Bailey, her owner hired her out to a series of temporary masters. First, Minty was hired out to James Cook, who

Marshes and hummocks of trees in southwestern Dorchester County where Minty Ross grew up. *Courtesy of James D. Hedberg.*

owned a nearby farm. She was sent into the marshes to tend his muskrat traps. At some point, Minty became sick with measles, but she was forced to continue working the traps anyway. She became so ill that she was sent back to her owner.[493]

Once her mother had nursed her back to health, Minty was hired out again. This time, she became a nursemaid and house servant to a young married woman who had been taught that slaves would not work unless you whipped them. The little girl was whipped repeatedly. She retained welts on her neck and shoulders from the beatings for the rest of her life.[494]

As a young teen, Minty Ross was nearly killed by a blow to her head from a two-pound weight that had been thrown by an angry overseer who was aiming at another slave. The weight hit Minty so hard that it drove a piece of the shawl she was wearing into her skull and knocked her unconscious.[495] For the rest of her life, she suffered from what was probably a form of epilepsy that produced headaches, seizures and sleeping spells that caused her to suddenly fall unconscious for minutes at a time.[496]

For five or six years, Minty Ross hired out to John T. Stewart, a Madison merchant and shipbuilder. Some owners allowed slaves to hire themselves out for a yearly fee. These slaves had the greatest chance of accumulating money to free themselves. In Minty's case, she used her savings to buy two steers and hired out both herself and her team of oxen.[497] She did many different jobs for Stewart—drove oxen, carted, plowed, hauled logs and worked in the woods.[498] Around 1844, Minty Ross married a free black man named John Tubman and took the name Harriet Tubman.

LOOKING NORTH TO FREEDOM

In 1849, Harriet Tubman's owner, Edward Brodess, died. Any time a slave owner died, slaves automatically became concerned that the division of the estate among the heirs and the payment of outstanding debts would result in the breakup of families and the sale of slaves.[499]

The greatest fear among Eastern Shore slaves in the 1840s was being sold South.[500] When her owner died, leaving many debts, Harriet may have feared that she, too, would end up in a slave market in Natchez or New Orleans. She did not wait to find out if her new owner, Eliza Brodess, would "sell her down the river."[501]

On September 17, 1849, Harriet Tubman ran away from the Anthony Thompson plantation with her brothers Ben and Henry. It was two weeks before Eliza Brodess finally realized that three of her slaves had run away and put this advertisement in the *Cambridge Democrat*.[502]

THREE HUNDRED DOLLARS REWARD.
RANAWAY from the subscriber on Monday the 17th ult [the previous month], *three negroes, named as follows: HARRY* [Henry], *aged about 19 years, has on one side of his neck a wen* [growth or tumor], *just under the ear, he is of a dark chestnut color, about 5 feet 8 or 9 inches hight; BEN, aged about 25 years, is very quick to speak when spoken to, he is of a chestnut color, about 6 feet high; MINTY, aged about 27 years, is of a chestnut color, fine looking, and about 5 feet high. One hundred dollars reward will be given for each of the above named negroes, if taken out of the State, and $50 each if taken in the State. They must be lodged in Baltimore, Easton or Cambridge Jail, in Maryland.*
ELIZA BRODESS
Near Bucktown, Dorchester county, Md. Oct. 3d, 1849.

Before these three runaways could be captured, however, Harriet's brothers got cold feet and decided to go back to the Thompson farm. They forced her to go back with them.[503]

Harriet did not stay long on the Thompson plantation. A few weeks later, she ran away again, this time by herself, escaping up the course of the Choptank River into Delaware and eventually into Philadelphia. Later, she said: "I had reasoned dis out in my mind; there was one of two things I had a *right* to, liberty or death; if I could not have one, I would have de oder; for no man should take me alive."[504]

Harriet's flight north required great courage. Most slaves on the Eastern Shore had very limited knowledge of the North. As Frederick Douglass noted: "The real distance [from Maryland to freedom] was great enough, but the imagined distance was, to our ignorance, much greater."[505]

The "known world" of the Eastern Shore slave was quite small. Some Eastern Shore slaves knew of Philadelphia; a few might have heard of New York, but probably none of them had any conception of Canada. And of course, in Philadelphia and New York, they still might be found by slave catchers and returned to slavery.

Runaway slaves on the Eastern Shore normally hid in the woods or marshes until their masters stopped looking for them. Then they followed the rivers into Delaware. Or they followed the map in the sky. They knew that the "drinking gourd" or Big Dipper could point them to Polaris, the North Star. And the North, they knew, meant freedom.[506]

On her second escape attempt, Harriet Tubman first got help from someone she later called "a sympathetic white woman." That woman was probably Hannah Leverton, a Quaker whose husband owned a local gristmill. She gave Harriet two names and directions to the first person who would point her way to the second.[507] These people were agents of the Underground Railroad.

By the time Harriet Tubman ran away, the Underground Railroad included safe houses in Delaware, Pennsylvania and New York where Eastern Shore runaway slaves could hide.[508] They then were moved from one household to another as they fled farther north. By day, escaping slaves were hidden in attics and haylofts or even in shocks of corn. By night, they were piloted through the woods or concealed in wagons until they got to the next safe house ten to twenty miles away.

In Philadelphia, Harriet Tubman was helped by William Still. She got work as a domestic servant and cook in various hotels in Philadelphia and in Cape May, New Jersey, saving her money with the intent of rescuing her family.[509]

Harriet Tubman, wood engraving by John G. Darby, 1868. *Courtesy of the National Portrait Gallery, Smithsonian Institution.*

Frontispiece and title page of William Still's *The Underground Railroad: A Record*, 1872. *Courtesy of Dr. Cassandra L. Newby-Alexander.*

William Still is one of the more interesting station masters of the Underground Railroad. His parents were born on Maryland's Eastern Shore. His father, Levin Still, bought his freedom in 1798 from his Caroline County master and moved to New Jersey. Still's mother, Charity, successfully escaped on her second attempt, taking with her their two daughters but forced to leave behind their two sons.[510]

In the early 1850s, William Still's Underground Railroad office in Philadelphia was aiding an average of sixty fugitives a month.[511] He interviewed all the slaves who came through his station and kept records that included names and descriptions of each runaway, as well as the name of the master.

Still's records include many accounts of escapes from the Eastern Shore. The stories that these fugitives told make it quite clear why slaves risked their lives to run away from their Eastern Shore owners.

Emory Roberts, one of Edward Lloyd's slaves from Talbot County, told Still that his master treated his slaves with "great severity." The lash was used freely "on women as well as men, old and young....Food and clothing...

were dealt out very stintedly, and daily suffering was the common lot of slaves under Lloyd." Emory fled to avoid a terrible flogging that he had been promised, leaving behind his wife, mother, brothers and sisters.[512]

Perry Johnson from Elkton in Cecil County had been severely flogged by both his master and his mistress. She had hit her slave so hard with a cowskin that he had lost one of his eyes. Perry described his mistress as a "perfect savage" who "was in the habit of cowhiding any of her slaves whenever she felt like it, which was quite often."[513]

Asbury Irwin from Kent County said, "I run away because I was used bad; three years ago I was knocked dead with an ax by master; the blood run out of my head as if it had been poured out of a tumbler."[514]

Ann Maria Green, a slave of Caroline County farmer James Pipper, said that her owner "was as mean a man as ever walked....He tried to work me to death, and treated me as mean as he could without killing me....I wish I had as many dollars as he has whipped me with sticks and other things."[515]

Solomon Light, a twenty-three-year-old slave from Cambridge, said his owner was an "unaccountable mean man" who would not allow his slaves enough to eat or sufficient clothing. Solomon had been told that he was going to be "sold South tomorrow."[516]

In total numbers, no one knows how many slaves were rescued by the Underground Railroad. The historian Fergus Bordewich estimated that as many as 100,000 were helped to freedom.[517] Regardless of numbers, the system thoroughly enraged and frustrated southern slaveholders, many of whom "suspected a conspiracy of abolitionists within their midst tempting slaves to run away."[518]

Once, Frederick Douglass had eleven Dorchester County fugitives in his attic in Rochester, New York. They had to stay hidden until he raised enough money to send them on to Canada. In his autobiography, he described his job for the Underground Railroad as fascinating and satisfactory work. "True, as a means of destroying slavery, it was like an attempt to bail out the ocean with a teaspoon, but the thought that there was **one** less slave, and one more freeman…brought to my heart unspeakable joy."[519]

COMPROMISE AND CONFLICT

While Harriet Tubman was moving north to freedom, the issue of the expansion of slavery reared its head again. The Missouri Compromise of

1820 had been merely a temporary bandage. Southern slave owners were still pressing to move slavery into the West. Northerners continued to balk at that idea.

In the summer of 1850, the year after Harriet Tubman ran away, Maryland officials were invited to attend a conference of the slave-owning states to discuss the possibility of secession from the United States. Governor Philip F. Thomas, however, declined the invitation to the Nashville Convention.[520] The enslaved population in Maryland had reached its peak in 1810, forty years earlier, and Governor Thomas thought that most Marylanders did not favor secession. Total numbers of slaves had declined over the years; by 1850, the size of the slave population by percent of the total had been cut in half—from 30 percent to 15 percent.[521]

TOTAL POPULATION	
1810	380,546
1820	407,350
1840	468,019
1850	583,033

SLAVES (% of total population)	
1810	**111,502 (30%)**
1820	107,397 (26%)
1840	89,737 (19%)
1850	90,368 (15%)

Left: CHART 6. TOTAL MARYLAND POPULATION, 1810–1850.
Right: CHART 7. SLAVE POPULATION IN MARYLAND, 1810–1850.

White, Free Black, and Slave Population on Maryland's Eastern Shore, 1790-1850

Jurisdiction	White			Free Black			Slave		
	1790	1850	Change	1790	1850	Change	1790	1850	Change
Caroline	7,028	6,096	-13.3%	421	2,788	+562%	2,057	808	-60.7%
Cecil	10,055	15,472	+53.9%	163	2,623	+1,509%	3,407	844	-75.3%
Dorchester	10,010	10,747	+7.4%	528	3,848	+629%	5,337	4,282	-19.8%
Kent	6,748	5,616	-16.8%	655	3,143	+380%	5,433	2,627	-51.6%
Queen Anne's	8,171	6,936	-15.1%	618	3,278	+430%	6,674	4,270	-36.0%
Somerset	8,272	13,385	+61.8%	268	3,483	+1,200%	7,070	5,588	-21.0%
Talbot	7,231	7,084	-2.0%	1,076	2,593	+141%	4,777	4,134	-13.5%
Worcester	7,626	12,401	+62.6%	178	3,014	+1,593%	3,836	3,444	-10.2%
Eastern Shore	65,141	77,737	+19.3%	3,907	24,770	+534%	38,591	25,997	-32.6%

Eastern Shore population statistics, 1790 and 1850. *Courtesy of the author.*

On the Eastern Shore, slave population had dropped from 38,591 in 1790 to 25,997—a 32.6 percent decline. Every county on the Shore had witnessed that decrease. The drop had been quite dramatic in Caroline County (60.7), Cecil County (75.3) and Kent County (51.6). In 1850, slaves represented only about a fifth of the area's population (20.2 percent), down from 35.9 percent of the total population in 1790.[522]

While slave numbers had declined, the population of free blacks on the Eastern Shore had soared 534 percent.

THE COMPROMISE OF 1850 AND THE FUGITIVE SLAVE ACT

Talk of secession in 1850 by some of the southern states was temporarily quieted by another complicated compromise. Designed by Henry Clay of Kentucky and promoted by Stephen A. Douglas of Illinois, the Compromise of 1850 was really five separate laws. California was to enter the Union as a free state. The rest of the territory taken from Mexico was to be organized without any action regarding slavery. The slave trade in the District of Columbia was abolished. Texas renounced its claim to New Mexico, with the United States assuming Texas's debt. And a stronger fugitive slave law was passed.[523]

It was the new Fugitive Slave Act that really riled up northerners. To put the new law in perspective, the Constitution, from the beginning, gave slave owners protection from runaway slaves. Article IV, Section 2 says, "No Person held to Service or Labour in one State…escaping into another, shall…be discharged from such Service or Labour, but shall be delivered up on Claim of the Party to whom such Service or Labour may be due."

In 1793, Congress passed a fugitive slave law that provided the mechanism by which this would be done. It said that if a master or his agent caught a runaway and swore to his identity before any magistrate, the judge then would issue a certificate of removal to return the slave to his owner.[524]

Professional slave catchers started kidnapping free blacks in the North and swearing that they were runaways. Consequently, northern states started passing "personal liberty laws" to protect their free blacks. When these laws were challenged, the Supreme Court ruled that *federal* law took precedence over *state* law and that states had no right to obstruct federal authorities who were enforcing the law. But, the court added, states were under no obligation to assist federal authorities. They did not have to catch or jail runaways or even hear their cases.[525]

In contrast, by the Fugitive Slave Act of 1850, the government made it a federal crime to not return fugitives to their rightful owners. Fines were levied of up to $1,000 and imprisonment of up to six months if a person was found guilty of helping a fugitive. If that help resulted in the loss of the slave, the guilty party had to pay the slave owner $1,000. Federal commissioners (who could issue certificates of removal) were to be appointed in every county in the United States. In court, if a slave catcher identified a free black as a runaway, the law stated, "In no trial or hearing under this act shall the testimony of such alleged fugitives be admitted in evidence." So, those accused could not even defend themselves. Now, no free black was safe from enslavement.[526]

Northern abolitionists were outraged by the new law. The New England poet Ralph Waldo Emerson mused: "This filthy enactment was made in the nineteenth century by people who could read and write. I will not obey it."[527] Frederick Douglass compared the 1850 Fugitive Slave law to game hunting. The act turned the United States, he said, into "a hunting ground for *men*."

Effects of the Fugitive-Slave-Law.

Courtesy of the Library of Congress.

Slaves have become "bird for the sportsman's gun." And all good citizens are commanded by your lawmakers "to engage in this hellish sport." "The right of the hunter to his prey stands superior…to *all* rights in this republic, the rights of God included!"[528]

Abolitionists in New York published a pictorial condemnation of the act titled "Effects of the Fugitive Slave Law." The illustration depicts four black men (who could be free) being ambushed in a cornfield by a group of white slave catchers (shown at the back). Two of the blacks have already been shot as they tried to flee. At the bottom of the lithograph are two quotations highlighting the immorality of Congress's action. One is the phrase from the Declaration of Independence that "all men are created equal," and the other is biblical:

Thou shalt not deliver unto the master his servant which has escaped from his master unto thee: He shall dwell with thee. Even among you in that place which he shall choose in one of thy gates where it liketh him best. Thou shalt not oppress him. Deuteronomy XXIII: 15-16

If enforced, the Fugitive Slave Act would destroy the Underground Railroad.

HARRIET TUBMAN—"THE MOSES OF HER PEOPLE"

In Maryland, in spite of the Fugitive Slave Act, Harriet Tubman risked returning to the area to rescue her niece Kessiah Bowley (her eldest sister's daughter) and Kessiah's children James and Araminta.

In December, Kessiah and her children were put on the auction block with a group of other slaves at the front of the Dorchester County Courthouse in Cambridge. Kessiah's husband was John Bowley, a free black sailor who had once worked for John T. Stewart. John Bowley outbid everyone. When the auctioneer appeared to collect payment at the end of the auction, however, no one came forward to pay; Kessiah and the children were missing. John Bowley had whisked them away and hidden them in a nearby house. Later that evening, he took them in his small boat and sailed for Baltimore. In Fells Point, they met Harriet, who was concealed at her brother-in-law Tom Tubman's house, and she led them safely to Philadelphia.[529]

Over the next eleven years, Harriet Tubman returned to Maryland twelve more times to rescue additional members of her family and to help other

Cambridge Courthouse, Dorchester County, Maryland, 2017. *Courtesy of James D. Hedberg.*

slaves escape to freedom. She personally led away about seventy slaves and also gave instructions to approximately fifty more who found their way to freedom independently.[530] Her first biographer, Sarah Bradford, called her "the Moses of her people."

Harriet Tubman was aided in her exploits by the long-established network of communication among African Americans in the communities where she had worked. Most black people on the Eastern Shore, whether they were slave or free, moved around according to the arrangements of the white families in the region. Some whites owned land and farms across great distances, even in different counties. So, at varying times throughout the year, they shifted their enslaved and hired black labor. Because of this shifting of the labor force, black families were forced to create an intricate web of communication in order to maintain ties with their family and friends.[531]

A few months after Kessiah Bowley and her children escaped, Harriet Tubman returned to Baltimore to help her brother Moses and two other men flee. Then she returned to Dorchester County to get her husband. In the two years since she had been gone, however, John Tubman had taken another wife, and he refused to leave the Eastern Shore. Harriet later told Sarah Bradford that while she was angry and hurt, she decided that if her husband could do without her, she could do without him—so she "dropped [him] out of her heart." She then gathered a group of slaves and led them to Philadelphia.[532]

In 1854, when Harriet learned that Eliza Brodess was planning to sell her brothers over the Christmas holiday, she again returned to Dorchester County. A literate friend in Philadelphia wrote a letter for her to send to Jacob Jackson, a free black living in Dorchester County who could read and write. Harriet requested that he read her letter "to the old folks, and give my love to them, and tell my brothers to be always watching unto prayer, and when the good old ship of Zion comes along, to be ready to step aboard." The letter was signed "William Henry Jackson," the name of Jackson's adopted son.[533]

Mail coming from the North (for whites as well as for blacks) was routinely examined, and postal authorities in Dorchester County were suspicious. They read Jackson's letter, but they could learn nothing from it. When they asked Jacob Jackson what it meant, he said, "[That] letter can't be meant for me, no how. I can't make head nor tail of it." He left the letter at the post

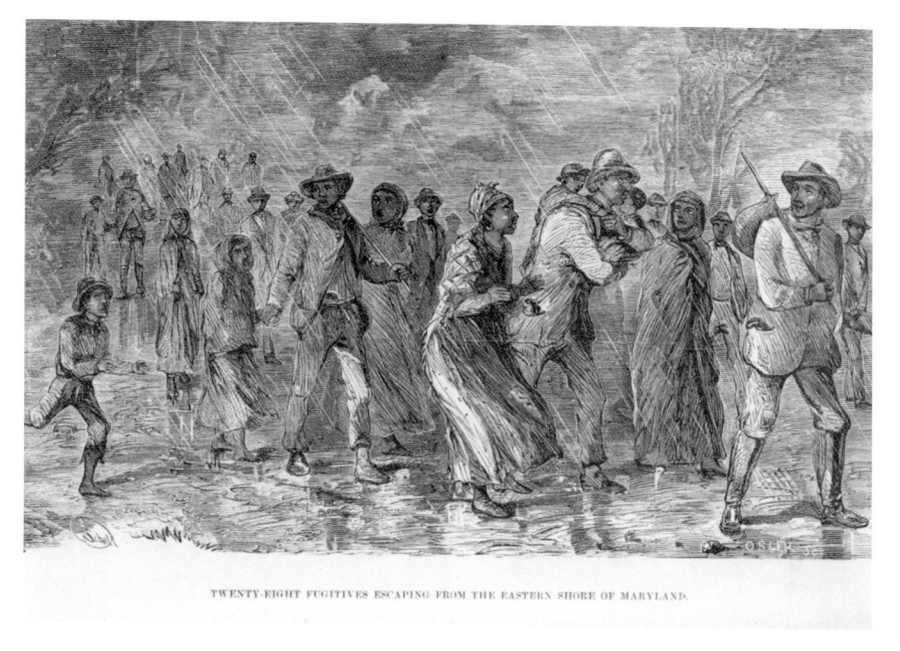

TWENTY-EIGHT FUGITIVES ESCAPING FROM THE EASTERN SHORE OF MARYLAND.

Courtesy of the Library of Congress.

office. But he let Harriet's brothers know that she was coming and that they had to be ready at a moment's notice to go with her.[534]

Thirty-five-year-old Robert, the eldest of Harriet's brothers, was married with three children (one, a new baby). Henry was also married and would be leaving his wife and two small children. Her brother Ben Jr. was planning to marry Jane Kane, a slave who lived on a nearby plantation. But Jane's owner refused to allow the two to wed. Ben arranged for Jane to disguise herself in men's clothing and flee with him to freedom.[535]

Harriet also often disguised herself in men's clothing or dressed like an elderly woman.[536] She usually organized her escapes on Saturday evenings. No newspapers were printed on Sunday, so advertisements for runaways could not run until Monday.[537] Slaves were often given travel privileges on weekends, so movement between farms would not look uncommon.[538] And she usually traveled at night. William Still wrote of Tubman:

> *Harriet was a woman of no pretensions, indeed, a more ordinary specimen of humanity could hardly be found among the unfortunate farmhands of the South. Yet, in point of courage, shrewdness and disinterested exertions to rescue her fellow-men…she was without her equal.*[539]

Harriet Tubman was convinced that she was a chosen agent of God, who guided her every act.[540] She said, "The Lord who told me to take care of my people meant me to do it just so long as I live, and so I do what he told me to do."[541]

Slaves other than those led by Harriet Tubman also were escaping from the Eastern Shore. On March 8, 1857, eight such slaves escaped from Dorchester County. Outside Dover, Delaware, a free black named Thomas Otwell betrayed the eight for reward money of $3,000. Otwell tried to convince the fugitives that the local sheriff was an abolitionist and that the Dover jail was a safe place to hide for the night. They became suspicious, jumped out of the second-floor window of the jail and escaped.[542]

There were rumors that Reverend Samuel Green, a highly respected, literate,

Reverend Samuel Green. *From William Still,* The Underground Railroad, *1872.*

free black Methodist minister, had helped the "Dover Eight."[543] The Dorchester County sheriff got a search warrant for Reverend Green's home in East New Market. There he found some New Jersey railroad schedules, a Canadian map, letters from some Dorchester County runaways who were living in Canada, a copy of the first volume of *Uncle Tom's Cabin* and a letter from the minister's son Samuel Green Jr.[544] (Sam Jr. was a slave who had escaped to Canada in 1853 with help from Harriet Tubman.)[545]

In 1841, the Maryland Assembly had enacted a law that read:

> *If any free negro or mulatto shall knowingly call for, demand, or receive, or have in his or her possession any abolition handbill, pamphlet, newspaper, pictorial representation or other paper of an inflammatory character, having a tendency to create discontent amongst or stir up to insurrection the people of color of this State…he or she shall be deemed guilty of a felony.*[546]

Reverend Green was found guilty of "having in his possession a certain abolition pamphlet called *Uncle Tom's Cabin*." For having a copy of that little book, this respected minister was sentenced to ten years in the Maryland Penitentiary.[547]

In 1857 (the year of the "Dover Eight" and Reverend Green's trial), Harriet Tubman learned that her father was at risk of arrest for aiding runaway slaves, so she returned to the Eastern Shore to rescue her parents. Harriet's father, Ben Ross, had been freed in 1840 by a provision in the will of his owner, Anthony Thompson. Thompson had also bequeathed to Ben ten acres of land on Poplar Neck in Caroline County to live on for the rest of his life and the privilege of cutting timber on that land. For an owner to provide this type of material support to a former slave was highly unusual.[548]

After Ben Ross was freed, he continued to work as a timber inspector for Joseph Stewart and his sons and for other men in the area who could use his skills. He also became an Underground Railroad agent, operating from his home on Poplar Neck.[549] In 1855, Ben Ross bought his wife, Ritta, from Eliza Brodess for twenty dollars. Part of the bill of sale reads, "By these presents do grant bargain and sell unto the said Benjamin Ross (Col'd man) his heirs and assigns the following negro woman named Ritty aged about 55 years slave for life and sound in body and mind."[550]

This document clearly says that Eliza Brodess attests to Ritta being a "slave for life." In fact, Rit already should have been free. Rit had originally belonged to Atthow Pattison. Pattison's 1797 will had specified that Rit was to be freed at age forty-five. By 1855, when her husband bought her, Harriet's mother was certainly much older than her owner claimed.[551]

When Harriet Tubman returned to the Eastern Shore to rescue her parents, she was aided by Thomas Garrett, a Quaker Underground Railroad station master in Wilmington, Delaware. By then, she had passed through Garrett's station many times.[552] This time, before she went south, Garrett gave Harriet both money and shoes. Ben and Ritta Ross and twenty-four others escaped on this Tubman trip to the Eastern Shore. Her parents eventually joined a community of Dorchester County ex-slaves living in St. Catharines, Canada.

Thomas Garrett used his own money to help over two thousand runaways over a thirty-year period. In 1860, Curtis W. Jacobs, a member of the House of Delegates from Worcester County, denounced Thomas Garrett as "wicked" for helping Eastern Shore slaves flee. He called Garrett "a base traitor to man and God." Jacobs introduced a resolution in the Maryland Assembly to have a $2,000 bounty given to any person who captured Garrett and had him jailed so that he could be tried and punished.[553]

THE "NEGRO QUESTION" AND BLACK CODES

Talk of abolition in the 1840s and '50s increasingly had raised the concern of many whites in Maryland that they might be forced to live in a society that included large numbers of blacks. As the rural free black population on the Eastern Shore grew, racism intensified. Whites began to worry that Maryland was "destined to be a free negro state."[554] Newspapers began to talk about the "Negro question" rather than the "slavery question."[555]

The 1860 census for Maryland showed that while 75 percent of the population was white, the state had a black population of 171,131. Of that population, there were just about as many free blacks as there were slaves.[556] But, the pie graph "Maryland's Population in 1860" does not tell the whole story. Examine the graph "Black Population of Maryland by Region in 1860."[557] (Regional percentages are across the top of the graph.) You can see from the statistics in that graph that "place" makes all the difference.

In the northern section of the state (which in this compilation means Baltimore City, Baltimore, Harford and Cecil Counties), blacks were only 14 percent of the region's total population. And slaves made up only 18 percent of that region's blacks. Contrast that to southern Maryland (Anne Arundel,

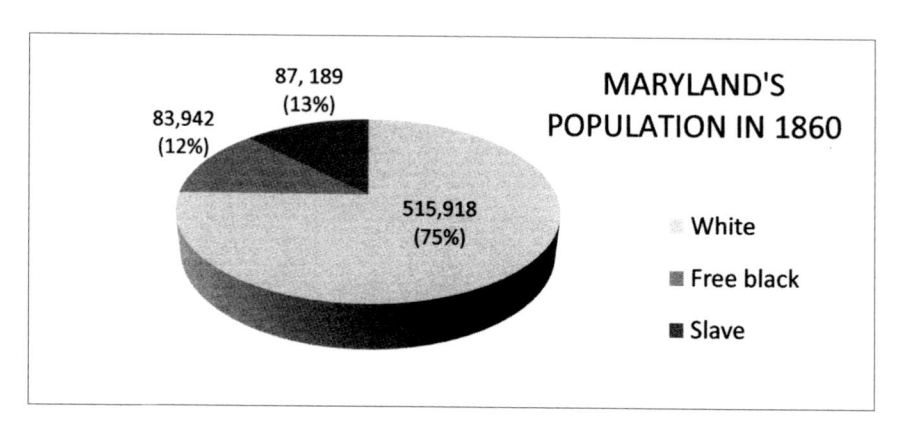

GRAPH 7. MARYLAND'S POPULATION IN 1860.

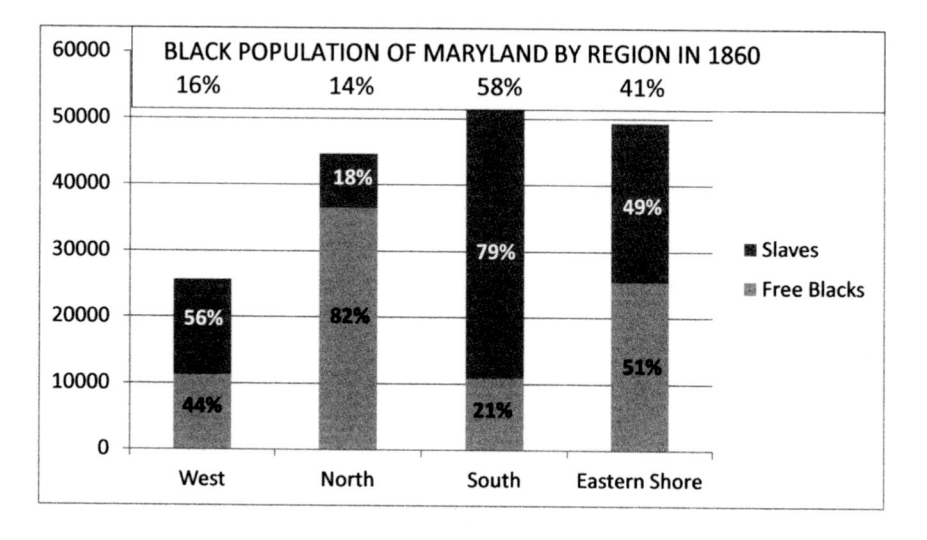

GRAPH 8. BLACK POPULATION OF MARYLAND BY REGION IN 1860.

Calvert, Charles, Prince George's and St. Mary's Counties). There, blacks made up 58 percent of the total population of the region (more than half), and 79 percent of those blacks were still enslaved.

The statistics for the Eastern Shore look different from either of those two areas. In 1860, the black population living on the Eastern Shore peninsula totaled 49,366. They made up about 41 percent of the population, and more than half of them were free. In 1860, two out of every five Shore residents were black. Queen Anne's County had a black population of 47 percent; Kent, a population of 45 percent. Cambridge, the major city in Dorchester County, was 56 percent black.[558]

In 1860, many on the Eastern Shore (as well as many in southern Maryland) believed that if blacks ever outnumbered whites, blacks would turn against their former masters.[559] That underlying fear influenced legislation.[560]

The term "black codes" is usually associated with laws passed in the South after the Civil War to deny equality to former slaves. In fact, as we have already seen, black codes are much older than that. In the 1830s, '40s and '50s, slave states already had constructed sets of harsh laws to proscribe the lives of blacks and distinguish them from white people.[561] In Maryland, a committee of the House of Delegates wrote in 1843: "Hardly a session of the legislature passes that some law is not enacted restricting them in their rights and privileges."[562]

Free blacks were prevented from moving around freely. They were required to register and carry "freedom papers," which could be challenged by any white. Free blacks could not participate in politics—they could neither vote nor hold office. They could not testify in court against a white. They could not work in certain trades or own a gun or a dog without permission. Free blacks could not assemble in groups or worship without a white minister present. And, they were punished for criminal acts far more severely than whites.[563]

Even the children of free blacks in Maryland suffered. In 1839, the Assembly had passed "An Act to provide for the better regulation of the Free Negro and Mulatto Children within the State." The law allowed the judge of the Orphans Court to take control of any colored child if he thought "it would be better for the habits and comfort of such child." The court then would bind the child as an apprentice to a white person, ostensibly "to teach habits of industry." Boys were apprenticed until they were twenty-one and girls until they were sixteen. And the sheriff was paid two dollars for each child he brought before the court.[564]

The Maryland legislature also passed vagrancy laws. Free blacks were arrested for minor infractions and then committed to involuntary labor. Those who could not pay fines and jail fees could be auctioned off for lengthy periods where they were essentially slaves. And authorities were totally unconcerned when groups of white vigilantes terrorized free blacks.

After 1860, in Maryland, manumission was no longer allowed; free blacks could not come into the state; police commissioners could sell or bind out free blacks who had been imprisoned. And free blacks above the age of eighteen actually were allowed to renounce their freedom and once again become slaves.[565] At this point, the only thing that distinguished a free black from a slave was the free black's right to own property and control his own time.[566]

Even though they had so few rights, free blacks still were considered a danger because they negated the underlying assumption upon which slavery was based.[567] If slavery was justified because black people were innately inferior and therefore unfit for freedom, how was it possible that free blacks had been able to fulfill contracts, buy land, create farms, organize churches and schools and save to buy freedom for their family members? Free blacks were undeniable proof of the slave owner's false reasoning.[568]

In spite of the obvious, Supreme Court chief justice Roger Brooke Taney essentially validated the slave owner's reasoning in 1857 when he declared in *Dred Scott v. Sandford* that since blacks were "beings of an inferior order, and altogether unfit to associate with the white race either in social or political relations," they had no rights "which the white man [was] bound to respect."[569] The court further ruled that the Missouri Compromise of 1820 was unconstitutional and that Congress could not prevent slave owners from taking their slaves wherever they wished. This decision meant both that slavery could exist wherever an owner took his slave and that free blacks had no legal rights anywhere.[570]

HARRIET, FREDERICK AND JOHN BROWN

By this time, Harriet Tubman's activities had piqued the interest of the radical abolitionist John Brown. Brown had gained notoriety in 1854 in the Kansas Territory when he and his sons murdered five pro-slavery farmers in what was called the Pottawatomie Massacre.[571] But a free Kansas was not John Brown's ultimate goal. He wanted to end slavery everywhere. After he left Kansas, John Brown decided to attack the federal arsenal at Harpers Ferry, Virginia, believing that this would show the slaves in the area that their supporters had come and slaves would desert their plantations en masse to join him.

In the spring of 1858, John Brown went to St. Catharines, Canada, to meet Harriet Tubman and, he hoped, recruit former Eastern Shore slaves to join his raid. He began to call Harriet "General." He wrote to his son (with no regard for sex): "He is the most of a man that I ever met with."[572] To Brown, Tubman stood apart—risking her life like few others he knew. He admired her self-control and her tolerance of extreme physical discomfort. Similarly, Brown was unlike any white man that Tubman had met before. He told her he had heard God's voice directing him and that it was time "for God's wrath to descend."[573] Harriet Tubman helped John Brown raise money in Boston in late May, but in the end, she did not join him, nor did any of the Dorchester County fugitives who listened to his plan when he met them at her house in the spring.

Frederick Douglass, who had known John Brown for almost a decade, met with him in a quarry near Chambersburg, Pennsylvania, in the summer of 1859. Douglass told Brown that his plan was doomed to failure. Douglass thought that an attack on a federal institution would turn the whole country against abolition.[574]

But Douglass's arguments did not persuade Brown to abandon the attack. On October 16, 1859 (two months after he met with Douglass), John Brown and a group of followers (fourteen white and five black) raided the federal arsenal at Harpers Ferry and proclaimed general emancipation. Brown had thought that once his attack began, blacks everywhere would come rallying to his support. That did not happen.[575]

Courtesy of the Library of Congress.

Brown and his men held out for more than thirty hours, but they were overpowered by U.S. troops under the command of Colonel Robert E. Lee. Brown was captured, found guilty of both treason and inciting slaves to insurrection and hanged.[576] News of "The Harpers Ferry Insurrection" quickly traveled throughout the United States via publications such as the popular *Frank Leslie's Illustrated Newspaper*.[577] Confiscation of John Brown's papers put many of the Underground Railroad conductors at risk. William Still hid his journals in a cemetery. Frederick Douglass and Harriet Tubman both fled to Canada, fearing that they would be arrested as co-conspirators.[578]

THE 1860 ELECTION, SECESSION AND WAR

In the 1860 presidential campaign, Republicans nominated Abraham Lincoln from Illinois on a platform opposing the further extension of slavery into the territories. Democrats split on the question of slavery. Northern Democrats nominated Stephen A. Douglas; southern Democrats nominated John C. Breckinridge. The Constitutional Union Party nominated John Bell of Tennessee and Edward Everett of Massachusetts. Its platform was "The Constitution of the Country, The Union of the States, and The Enforcement of the Laws." Constitutional Unionists said that there was no East, no West, no North and no South—nothing but the Union. They hoped to avoid secession by taking no stand about slavery, either for or against it.[579]

The Eastern Shore (except for Talbot and Worcester Counties) voted for John Bell. The total popular vote in Maryland in the 1860 election went to Breckinridge by eight-tenths of a percentage point. He won the state by just 722 votes.[580]

On December 20, 1860, as a protest against the election of Lincoln, South Carolina adopted the Ordinance of Secession. Within five months, ten other states had followed South Carolina's example.

The principal goal and purpose of secession and the Confederacy was to maintain slavery and white supremacy. Jefferson Davis, who became president of the Confederate States of America, had made that quite clear ten years earlier in the Senate's debate about the Compromise of 1850 when he defended slavery. He had said that Africans were destined to be enslaved and that fact was "immutable and eternal." Slavery had been "established by decree of Almighty God." It was recognized in the Bible and practiced throughout history.[581]

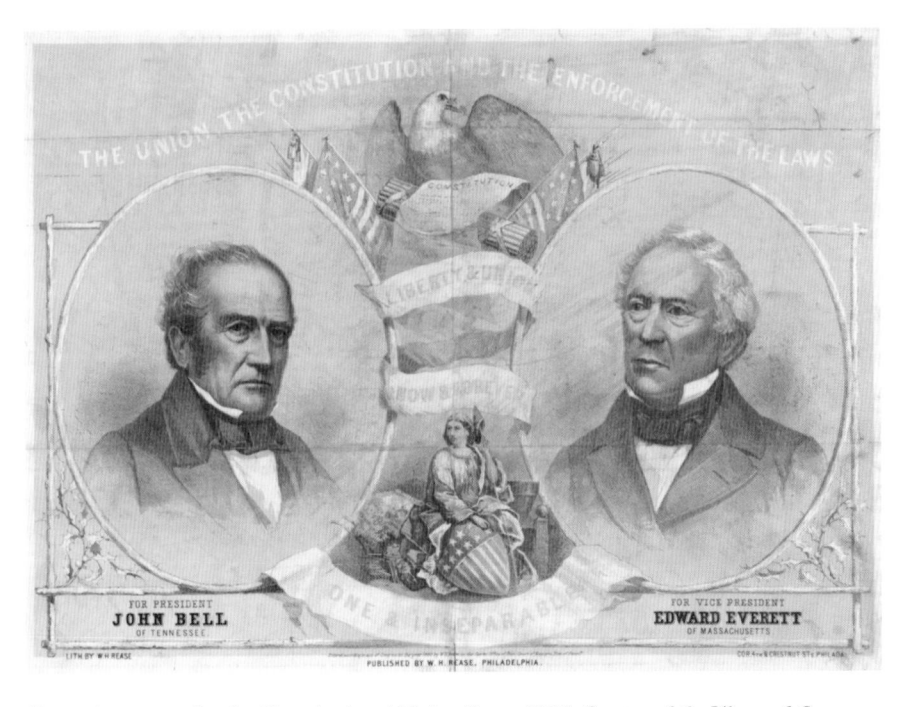

Campaign poster for the Constitutional Union Party, 1860. *Courtesy of the Library of Congress.*

Confederate vice president Alexander Stephens made the principles of the Confederacy even more clear in a speech he delivered in Savannah, Georgia, on March 21, 1861, when he said:

> *Our new government is founded upon exactly* [this] *idea; its foundations are laid, its cornerstone rests, upon the great truth, that the negro is not equal to the white man; that slavery—subordination to the superior race— is his natural and normal condition. This, our new government, is the first, in the history of the world, based upon this great physical, philosophical, and moral truth.*[582]

Slavery had been maintained by violence, and in the end, undoing slavery required violence as well.[583] In mid-April 1861, a month after Lincoln was inaugurated, South Carolinians fired on Federal troops at Fort Sumter in Charleston Harbor. In the North, news of the incident galvanized the population. Thousands in New York thronged Union Square to "rally 'round the flag." The president called upon the states to provide seventy-five thousand volunteer troops to protect the Union. The War Department was swamped with offers of thousands more.[584]

Marylanders were divided over which side of the conflict to support. Some fought for the Union. In September, the First Eastern Shore Regiment was organized at Cambridge with three companies in Dorchester County, four in Caroline, one in Talbot and one in Somerset. (Seven men from Hoopers Island joined that regiment.) Later in the year, the Second Eastern Shore Regiment was organized at Chestertown.[585]

Other Eastern Shoremen headed south to fight for the Confederacy. Governor Thomas Hicks, himself a Dorchester County native, asked the Federal government for arms and supplies to help root out "the secessionists that are now passing in great numbers through to the Eastern Shore of Virginia," where they were joining Confederate regiments.[586]

BLACKS IN THE CIVIL WAR

Over 200,000 black men served as soldiers and sailors in the Federal army and navy during the Civil War.[587] Free blacks like Josiah Cornish of Cambridge enlisted. He served in Company D of the Fourth Regiment, fighting in Virginia and North Carolina, where he was wounded several times.[588]

Eastern Shore slaves also served. By the Militia Act of 1862, Congress freed Rebel-owned slaves and their families when a slave enlisted in the Union army.[589] Loyal slaveholders were paid $100 for each slave who was recruited. To collect, slave owners had to produce papers freeing the recruited slave.[590]

Over one hundred slaves from the Eastern Shore enlisted (with their owners being paid). Among them were Robert Stafford, a sawyer who was enslaved to Caleb Shepherd; William Smith, a literate slave who belonged to William Radcliffe; George Jolley of Cambridge, who belonged to John R. Clayton; Robert Barnes, who was owned by John Dunnock of Meekins Neck; and Robert Bennett, one of the many slaves owned by William T. Goldborough of Horn's Point. These men served mainly in Virginia and North Carolina in the Seventh Regiment of the United States Colored Troops. Many were wounded; most returned to the Eastern Shore after the war was over.[591]

About forty-three thousand black soldiers died in battle or from disease during the Civil War. Black Union soldiers who were captured by Confederate troops were often returned to slavery. Many were executed immediately rather than taken prisoner.[592]

Frederick Douglass became a recruiting agent for the Fifty-Fourth Massachusetts Infantry, the first regiment of black soldiers raised in the North. His sons Charles and Lewis enlisted.[593] Harriet Tubman went to South Carolina, where she served the Union army as a nurse, scout, cook, recruiting agent and spy. Historian Fergus Bordewich asserts she was the first woman in American history to lead a detachment of troops into battle.[594]

THE EMANCIPATION PROCLAMATION AND MARYLAND'S CONSTITUTION OF 1864

In September 1862, President Lincoln announced that on January 1, 1863, all slaves in areas that were at war with the United States would be free. Lincoln's Emancipation Proclamation did not free slaves who lived in border states like Maryland, but it did set an example for what was to happen after the war was over.

Maryland did not wait for the hostilities to end. A new Constitution was passed in October 1864, making Maryland the first border state to free its slaves.[595] As of November 1, 1864, all slaves in Maryland were free.

On the Eastern Shore, only Caroline, Talbot and Worcester Counties supported the idea of holding a Constitutional Convention in 1864.[596] The Shore was equally divided over the major issue to be addressed at that convention—the freeing of Maryland's slaves.

The debate over Article 23, which would free the slaves, makes for fascinating reading. It fills over one hundred pages of the Constitutional Convention's records. In it, the representatives discuss everything from slavery in Greece and Rome to whether the Bible did or did not condone slavery. Some delegates saw slavery as more terrible than the Spanish Inquisition and the prime cause of the Civil War. Other delegates still thought blacks were mentally inferior and needed to be enslaved.[597] Eastern Shore delegates to the convention illustrate that split in opinion.

James Valliant from Talbot County, who described himself as "a plain, unvarnished, unsophisticated farmer," called slavery "an ebony idol" that the people of the South had bowed down to for generations. He declared:

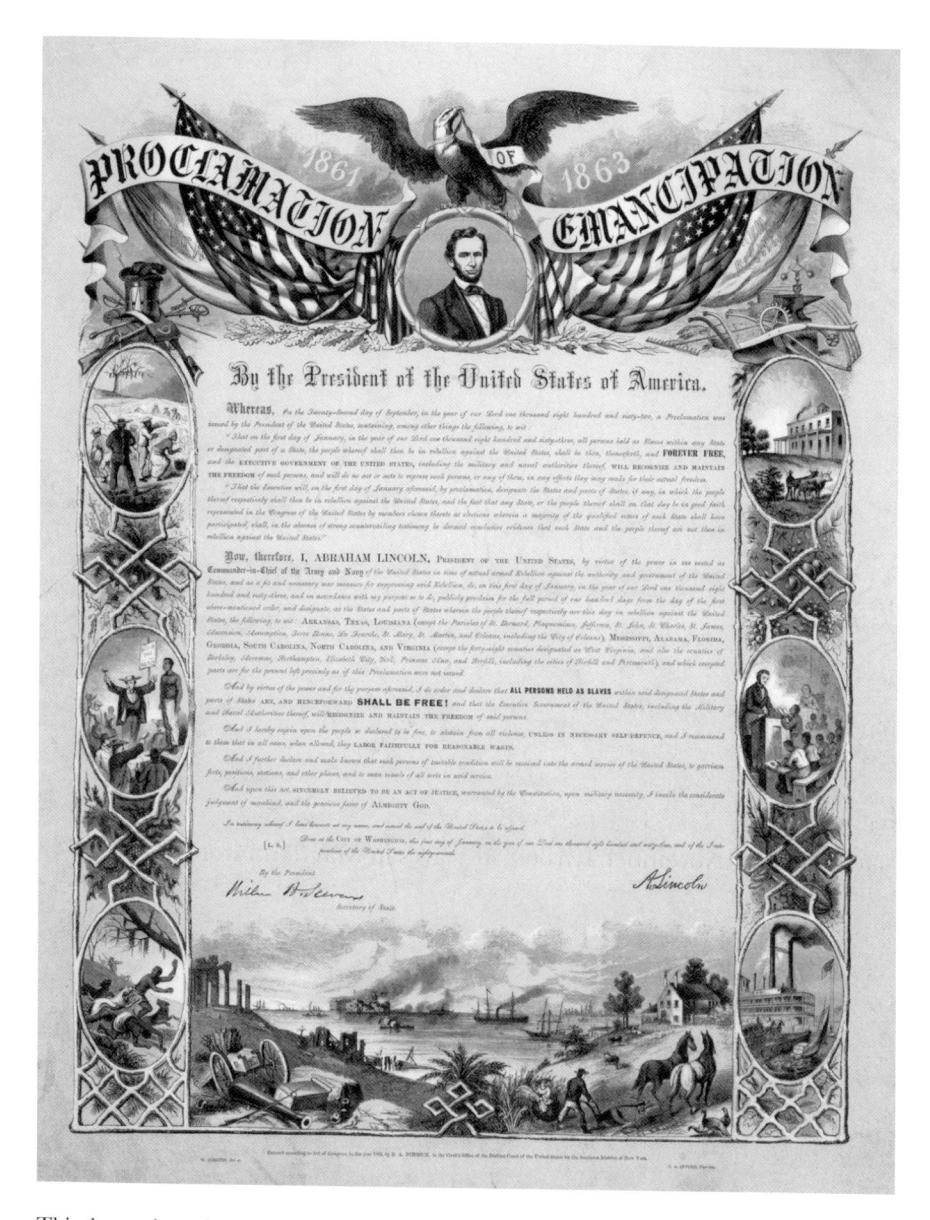

This decorative print was produced in 1864 to commemorate Lincoln's historic edict. *Courtesy of the National Portrait Gallery, Smithsonian Institution.*

The institution of slavery, as it exists in the American States, is not necessary to the good of any party, either the negro or the white man, and is only suffered for the benefit of the few, and this sufferance is at the expense of the many.… [Slavery] *is a moral evil, and for that reason, if for no other, it ought to be abolished.*[598]

Isaac D. Jones of Somerset County saw the issue differently. To him, slaves were private property, "not only recognized by the States, not only recognized by the Constitution of the United States…but, as I have already said, it is recognized by the law of nations." Jones thought that freeing the slaves would increase crime, pauperism and vice; ruin production and commerce; and cause blacks to quickly relapse "into his original African savagism." He went on to summarize his opposition to abolition, saying: "To overthrow the present relation of the races, is to injure both the white man and the negro, and to inflict a deadly blow upon the cause of humanity, civilization, and Christianity."[599]

In the end, however, in spite of pleas like those of Isaac Jones, the vote of the convention delegates was two to one in favor of the antislavery article: 53–27. Delegates from Talbot, Worcester and Caroline Counties supported emancipation. Those from Dorchester, Kent, Queen Anne's and Somerset opposed it.[600]

While the new Constitution emancipated the slaves of Maryland, it did not enfranchise them. And even then, the new Constitution was barely ratified. Citizens voting in their home precincts rejected the proposed Constitution by almost two thousand votes (29,536 to 27,541). However, because Maryland's Union soldiers voted overwhelmingly in favor of it—2,633 votes to 263—the 1864 Constitution became law.[601]

After five bloody years, the Civil War ended. Then, on April 15, 1865, five days after General Robert E. Lee surrendered, President Lincoln was assassinated. Andrew Johnson, Lincoln's vice president, became president.

On December 18, 1865, the Thirteenth Amendment to the Constitution was passed, prohibiting slavery within the United States. In 1866, Congress passed a Civil Rights Bill over President Johnson's veto. It declared all persons born in the United States to be citizens and entitled to equality under the law. The Fourteenth Amendment, ratified in 1868, incorporates those ideas into the Constitution. In 1869, the Fifteenth Amendment was ratified. It provides that the right to vote cannot be abridged because of "race, color, or previous condition of servitude."

The Maryland Assembly *rejected* both the Fourteenth and Fifteenth Amendments.[602]

Left: Frederick Douglass, 1870; *Right*: Harriet Tubman, early 1870s. *Courtesy of the Library of Congress.*

In 1869, Frederick Douglass's brother Perry Bailey moved back to the Eastern Shore from Rochester, New York.[603] He did not return to a place that welcomed blacks with open arms. Prejudice against color remained strong on the Eastern Shore. Two years later, the Lloyds entertained Jefferson Davis at Wye House. To some Eastern Shoremen, the Confederacy never died.

Frederick Douglass again visited the Eastern Shore in 1877. He even had a meeting in St. Michaels with his eighty-two-year-old former master Thomas Auld. Auld told him: "Frederick, I always knew you were too smart to be a slave, and had I been in your place, I should have done as you did."[604] In 1895, after an illustrious career as an orator, journalist and diplomat, Frederick Douglass died at his home in the District of Columbia. He was buried in Rochester, New York, beside his first wife.[605]

After the Civil War, Harriet Tubman settled on a small piece of property on the outskirts of Auburn, New York (west of Syracuse). She became active in the suffragette movement, and she founded a home for the elderly near where she lived. Harriet Tubman, the last of the great Underground Railroad conductors, died of pneumonia in 1913.

IN SUMMARY

In this final chapter, we have primarily dealt with the two decades just before the Civil War. In that period, the Eastern Shore became a two-caste society, as almost all the rights that free blacks at one time had enjoyed were taken away. Abolition movements failed because slave owners still controlled the Maryland legislature and because free blacks rejected immigration to Liberia. Hundreds of Eastern Shore slaves ran away, many helped by the Underground Railroad.

The country divided over the expansion of slavery issue, and that irreparable division led to the Civil War. Maryland sympathies were divided, with men fighting for both the Union and the Confederacy. Blacks, both free and slave, fought in the war.

While Maryland freed its slaves by the Constitution of 1864, freedom did not erase racial prejudice. The sad, continuing legacy of slavery on Maryland's Eastern Shore is that the views that most whites had formed about blacks before the Civil War as lazy, dishonest, untrustworthy burdens on society continued long after the slaves' freedom had been won.[606]

EPILOGUE

In these few chapters, I have written about slavery and race relations in one small corner of the world. But I do not want anyone reading this account to think that what happened on the Eastern Shore of Maryland has no connection to them personally because their ancestors did not own any slaves or because their ancestors did not come to the United States until after the Civil War.

Slavery was central to the world's economy for over 250 years. In that time, it was not just their owners who profited from the labor of slaves.[607] Hundreds of shipbuilders and sailors, from the Hanseatic ports of northern Europe to the shipyards of New England, benefited from slavery.[608] Bankers in the United States and in Europe, who made money on the credit they provided to slave owners, benefited from slavery.[609] Industrialists who made their fortunes from processing raw cotton and sugar cane benefited from slavery.[610] Companies like Aetna that insured slaves as property benefited from slavery.[611]

And if all your ancestors were ordinary Joes and Janes, they, too, benefited from slavery—when they wore soft cotton clothing rather than rough wool, when they sweetened their tea with sugar or when they enjoyed tobacco in their pipes. So, slavery has a connection to all of us.

While working on this project, I was told more than once that we should not judge our ancestors because they lived in a different age. I disagree. Fundamental ideas of right and wrong and what is fair are older than America, and there is a morality higher than written law. Thomas Auld,

Eliza Brodess, my own Hoopers Island ancestors and all the other slave owners (no matter where they lived, how many slaves they owned or how they treated their slaves) were wrong.

My study of race relations on the Eastern Shore of Maryland has brought me to the conclusion that blacks, both slave and free, are among the heroes of American history. Blacks survived the Middle Passage from Africa. They had their families torn apart by the internal slave trade. They labored to make our country's economy prosper, whether they slaved to grow tobacco, rice, sugar or cotton. Blacks have served in all of America's wars, fighting for a country that did not appreciate their sacrifices. And they have contributed positively to every aspect of American life—art, music, sports, medicine, literature, education, science, mathematics and religion—while courageously facing racial slurs, lynchings, red-lining, segregated facilities and Jim Crow.

In August 2017, as Baltimoreans debated whether or not to remove the city's Confederate monuments, one citizen wrote in a letter to the *Baltimore Sun*: "It [slavery] happened a very long time ago and did not affect anyone who is living today."[612] Sadly, that statement is far from true.

In the 1930s, Will Johnson, a black laborer on Hoopers Island, was able to buy a sandwich at only one of the community's six general stores. In 1963, a white restaurant owner in Cambridge broke eggs over the heads of blacks who were peacefully waging a sit-in on the sidewalk in front of his restaurant. In 1967 (more than a dozen years after *Brown v. Board of Education*), more than half the counties on the Eastern Shore of Maryland still had many segregated schools.[613] And in 2008, all up and down the Shore, people pronounced, "There is no way I am voting for a black man."

All of those actions are the result of racial attitudes that developed on the Eastern Shore peninsula hundreds of years ago and did not die. They are a part of the legacy of slavery.

Our country will never be able to atone for what we have done to our black population. The least we can do is to educate ourselves about the facts of our own history so that we have a truthful understanding of our past. When President Barack Obama dedicated the African American Museum in Washington, D.C., on September 24, 2016, he said that "a clear-eyed view of history can make us uncomfortable; but, because of that discomfort, we learn and grow." I learned an immense amount in preparing this history—about slavery, about the Eastern Shore, about my own family. Much of what I learned made me extremely uncomfortable. But I think this knowledge has helped me grow. I hope that those who have read this account have learned and grown as well.

NOTES

Chapter 1: Colonial Maryland to 1750

1. Berlin, *Generations of Captivity*, 60; Stevenson, *What Is Slavery?*. Stevenson's thesis is that slavery is based on power and supported by the mythology of racial superiority.
2. Berlin, *Slaves without Masters*, xv, states that many historians have ignored "both time and place" in their studies of the South—either treating long segments of time as one unit or describing the South as monolithic and making little or no distinction between the Upper South and the Deep South.
3. Berlin, *Many Thousands Gone*, 8. A similar distinction is made by John Hope Franklin and Alfred A. Moss Jr. in *From Slavery to Freedom*, 28. These authors speak of "old" slavery as a manifestation of wealth and later versions of the institution when slavery itself "was the foundation on which wealth was built."
4. Berlin, *Many Thousands Gone*, 8.
5. Berlin, *Generations of Captivity*, 9, suggests that the cruel and callous treatment might have been from people who treated all their subordinates that way—whether those subordinates were servants, debtors or the poor in general.
6. "During these first forty years [circa 1620–60] some free Negroes enjoyed the full fruit of the new rich land. They earned money, accumulated property, and occasionally held minor offices." Berlin, *Slaves without Masters*, 4.

7. Berlin, *Generations of Captivity*, 9.

8. Berlin, *Many Thousands Gone*, 9.

9. Ibid.; Bordewich, *Bound for Canaan*, 107, notes that slave owners believed "that bondage was ordained in the natural and God-given order of things." Some could not understand why slaves would want to be free.

10. The Eastern Shore has nine counties—Cecil, Kent, Queen Anne's, Talbot, Caroline, Dorchester, Somerset, Wicomico and Worcester. For this account, however, it has only eight counties. Wicomico County is a post–Civil War creation.

11. Thomas, *Slave Trade*, 56.

12. Berlin, *Generations of Captivity*, 18.

13. Thomas, *Slave Trade*, 83, 93; Stevenson, *What Is Slavery?*, 25.

14. Thomas, *Slave Trade*, 112. People of all classes owned slaves in Europe, and slaves could be found in France and Italy as well as in Portugal and Spain. In 1550, Lisbon had 10,000 slaves in a population of 100,000.

15. Berlin, *Generations of Captivity*, 32, says that New Amsterdam and Elmina were essentially the same type of settlements except for the fact that the New World colony was smaller and had a colder climate. By 1682, Elmina had a population between fifteen and twenty thousand and was the largest of the European centers in the area. Berlin, *Many Thousands Gone*, 19, 22.

16. By 1448, approximately one thousand slaves had been carried to Portugal or its islands—Madeira, Canaries, Azores, Cape Verde Islands and São Tomé. Thomas, *Slave Trade*, 59.

17. Ibid., 87. January 22, 1510. In the early years, the slave trade required special permission—the *asiento*. The crown both controlled and benefitted from the trade.

18. Sublette and Sublette, *American Slave Coast*, 75–76.

19. Berlin, *Generations of Captivity*, 44.

20. Founded in 1738 as Gracia Real de Santa Teresa de Mose, the Fort Mose (pronounced Moh-Say) settlement of about one hundred Africans was legally sanctioned by the Spanish Crown.

21. Letter from John Rolfe to Sir Edwin Sandys of the Virginia Company, quoted in Sublette and Sublette, *American Slave Coast*, 100.

22. Yeardley's plantation was named "Flowerdew Hundred." Stevenson, *What Is Slavery?*, 58.

23. Berlin, *Generations of Captivity*, 34.

24. Captain John Smith of Jamestown was a white man enslaved by the Tatars. Berlin, *Making of African America*, 54. Slavery in continental Europe was usually connected to domestic service, not the field.

25. Smith, "Minty's Legacy," 7–8. Smith notes that without the legal doctrine of *partus sequitur ventrum*, the children who resulted from the rape of enslaved women by their white owners would have been free. In her autobiography, Harriet Jacobs notes that "slaveholders have been cunning enough to enact that 'the child shall follow the condition of the mother,' not the father; thus taking care that licentiousness shall not interfere with avarice." Jacobs, *Incidents in the Life*, 117–18.

26. Radoff, "Settlement," 2.

27. Brugger, *Maryland*, 4, 5. The two neighboring colonies continued to fight over boundaries for years. See also Radoff, "Settlement," 3.

28. "The metes and bounds" described in Article III are quoted in Radoff, "Settlement," 4.

29. Carr, "Sources of Political Stability," 53–54.

30. Lord Baltimore offered his original investors a two-thousand-acre manor for every five settlers imported into the colony. In 1634, he reduced the amount of the grant to one thousand acres for every five who immigrated. Still later, the grant became one hundred acres for each settler and an additional fifty acres for each member of the family brought with him. Carr, Menard and Walsh, *Robert Cole's World*, 5.

31. Originally, land could be purchased at the rate of 200 pounds of tobacco for every 100 acres of land. That purchase price gradually increased until it peaked in 1738 at £5 sterling per 100 acres. Newton D. Mereness, *Maryland as a Proprietary Province* (New York, 1901), 50–51, 77, cited in Land, "Colonial Period," 13.

32. Radoff, "Settlement," 8.

33. Brugger, *Maryland*, 5–6.

34. The charter gave Calvert absolute control of ten to twelve million acres. Carr, "Sources of Political Stability," 53–54.

35. As a symbol of his fealty to the English king, Lord Baltimore was required to make an annual tribute of two Indian arrows. Brugger, *Maryland*, 12.

36. For an explanation of the operations of the colonial judicial system and the system of local government in the colony see Carr, "Sources of Political Stability," 44–70.

37. Dorchester County did not receive a charter government until 2002. As of June 6, 2017, Somerset County was still governed by county commissioners. See msa.maryland.gov.

38. Brugger, *Maryland*, 22, 23. There also were epidemics of influenza between 1675 and 1677 and smallpox in 1685 and 1686.

39. Henry Callister to William Whitfield, August 1, 1743, Henry Callister Papers, Maryland Diocesan Library on deposit at the Maryland Historical Society, in Tyler, "Foster Cunliffe and Sons," 253.

40. By 1642, over 500 people had immigrated to the Maryland colony, but only 340 to 390 were still alive. In 1648, the population of the colony was actually smaller than it had been in 1642. "Seasoning" had taken its toll. Chapelle, et al., *Maryland*, 14, 21; Brugger, *Maryland*, 23–24, gives a number of statistics about life expectancy in the colony, concluding with this dramatic statement: "Roughly half the children born in seventeenth-century Maryland died before reaching age twenty."

41. Berlin, *Making of African America*, 77. Perhaps as many as one-quarter to one-third of newly arrived African slaves died within the first year, many from diseases to which they had no resistance.

42. Berlin, *Many Thousands Gone*, 41.

43. Library of Congress, "An Advertisement for the Sale of Slaves, 1784," https://tse2.mm.bing.net/th?id=OIP.3-v90VO6Xhe3-Jrw70tdGwAAAA&pid=Api.

44. Brugger, *Maryland*, 43. Father White later imported another mulatto servant named Francisco.

45. Richard Kemp wrote to the Maryland governor in 1638 that he had brought "10 negroes for your lordship's use." Scharf, *History of Maryland*, 66, quoted in Thomas, *Slave Trade*, 177.

46. Browne, Papenfuse, et al., eds., *Archives of Maryland Online* 1:41 [hereafter *Archives MD*]. This series is ongoing and available online at http://www.msa.md.gov, where volumes, collectively or individually, can be searched electronically.

47. "Judicial and Testamentary Business of the Provincial Court, 1637–1650," *Archives MD* 4:189.

48. De facto slavery preceded law by at least twenty years. Kimmel, "Free Blacks in Seventeenth Century Maryland," 20.

49. Karinen, "Maryland Population 1634–1730," 383, 385.

50. "Patent Records," *Archives MD* S1426. "Hoopers Clifts" was patented in 1658 (Liber Q/folio 239).

51. Rountree and Davidson, *Eastern Shore Indians*, 84–93.

52. King Charles I bought silk-lined beaver hats for his entire retinue, so the hats became a symbol of status. Sublette and Sublette, *American Slave Coast*, 113.

53. "Judicial and Testamentary Business of the Provincial Court, 1637–1650," *Archives MD* 4:214. The judge found that John Hollis, the

plaintiff, should recover 677 pounds of tobacco for 67 arm-lengths of Roanoke and 1,350 pounds of tobacco for 13 pounds of beaver. Quotation from "General Assembly, January 1637/8–September 1664," *Archives MD* 1: 307.

54. There already had been settlement in the northern Shore with an administrative unit there named Kent County. Originally, the whole population of the county lived on Kent Island. See Karinen, "Maryland Population 1634–1730," 380.

55. Ibid., 398, 399.

56. Ibid., 393, 395. In general, new counties were formed when there were four hundred to five hundred inhabitants located in an area some distance from a court.

57. Thomas, *Slave Trade*, 89.

58. In the first half of the sixteenth century, upward of 2,500 natives—mostly women and children—were shipped to the Iberian Peninsula (a "reverse Middle Passage"). Reséndez, *Other Slavery*, 13, 48.

59. Brugger, *Maryland*, 9. Calvert made this exchange with the Indians "in order to avoid every appearance of injustice, and afford no opportunity for hostility." Radoff, "Settlement," 8. In the rest of the colony, the English generally ignored the rights to ownership of Native Americans who had lived on the land for thousands of years. Rountree and Davidson, *Eastern Shore Indians*, 100.

60. Archaeological evidence indicates that some Yaocomacoes, Indians from the western shore, hunted on the Eastern Shore on Barren Island just west of Hoopers Island across Tar Bay.

61. Mullikin, "Eastern Shore," 151.

62. "Proceedings of the Council of Maryland, 1636–1667," *Archives MD* 3:362–63.

63. Robinson, "Conflicting Views on Landholding," 89.

64. "General Assembly, April 1666–June 1676," *Archives MD* 2:200.

65. Three bands of Choptank Indians lived on their reservation—the Ababco, Hatsawap and Tequassino—probably each living in its own location. Rountree and Davidson, *Eastern Shore Indians*, 128.

66. Ibid., 143, 144. Into the early eighteenth century, the status of Indians was more closely equivalent to that of whites than to blacks.

67. Ibid., 165.

68. Land, in "Colonial Period," 17, sees the emphasis on tobacco as a negative for the colony since Maryland, with its single-crop economy, was "at the mercy of world prices of tobacco."

69. Neill, *Terra Mariae*, 199. Middleton, in *Tobacco Coast*, 42, posits that the Chesapeake Bay's configuration was of primary importance to establishing the tobacco economy. Carr, Menard and Walsh, in *Robert Cole's World*, 13, see tobacco as the only crop with "a fully developed marketing network extending from the Chesapeake Bay to England."

70. Middleton, *Tobacco Coast*, 107. "Tobacco exports rose from about thirty million pounds in the 1720s to one hundred million pounds by the 1770s," Brugger, *Maryland*, 58.

71. "Council of Maryland, 1698–1731," *Archives MD* 25:602.

72. Carr, Menard and Walsh, *Robert Cole's World*, 37.

73. Middleton, *Tobacco Coast*, 111. A bed of about fifty square yards produced enough plants for an acre. Carr, Menard and Walsh, *Robert Cole's World*, 54.

74. Seedlings were ready to be transplanted when the plants had four leaves. Berlin, *Many Thousands Gone*, 31.

75. This operation required great skill and was assigned to a trained servant or slave. Middleton, *Tobacco Coast*, 111.

76. Carr, Menard and Walsh, *Robert Cole's World*, 60.

77. Ibid., 63. Sweet-scented tobacco was grown primarily on the banks of the James, York, Rappahannock and Potomac Rivers. Middleton, *Tobacco Coast*, 109.

78. In the seventeenth century, hogsheads weighed between 400 and 800 pounds. In the course of the eighteenth century, because of bigger barrels and tighter packing, hogsheads of Oronoco might weigh between 750 and 1,150 pounds. Middleton, *Tobacco Coast*, 113.

79. "An Act for amending the Staple of Tobacco, for preventing Frauds in his Majesty's Customs, and for the Limitation of Officers Fees" is a complex piece of legislation that covers issues ranging from building warehouses in each county to keeping poor tobacco from Pennsylvania and Delaware out of the colony. "General Assembly, 1745–1747," *Archives MD* 44: 595–638. Virginia had had such an inspection law since 1730.

80. Statistics taken from Table 1: Estimated Population of Maryland, 1640–1730 in Menard, "Population, Economy, and Society," 72. Population growth, which was slow in the early years of the colony, increased significantly after 1660 due to the settlers' natural increase but also due to the immigration that Lord Baltimore encouraged. See Land, "Colonial Period," 16.

81. Indentured servants in the seventeenth century cost £15 to £20; able-bodied slave field hands sold for between £25 and £30 sterling depending on age and sex. Land, "Colonial Period," 22.

82. Menard, "Population, Economy, and Society," 86. The term of indenture was usually four to five years. Brugger, *Maryland*, 16. Some indentured servants were black. After 1718, convict indenture was seven years' colonial servitude for non-capital offenses and fourteen years for felonies for which execution was mandatory. Middleton, *Tobacco Coast*, 166.

83. "Patent Records," *Archives MD*: Liber AB&H/folio 140. On July 15, 1653, Henry Hooper of Patuxent claimed land before "Mr. Richard Preston, Commander and his Lordship's Surveyor Generale," for transporting himself, his family and Sarah Watson, John Taylor and Robert Stiles.

84. Middleton, in *Tobacco Coast*, 168, states that more than twenty thousand convicts were brought to the Chesapeake during the eighteenth century—two-thirds of the total number sent to America.

85. Ibid., 161. In the 1620–60 period when the English government was in turmoil, tens of thousands of indentured servants immigrated to North America. Blackburn, *American Crucible*, 61.

86. Berlin, *Generations of Captivity*, 31.

87. Berlin, *Many Thousands Gone*, 110. Middleton, *Tobacco Coast*, 149–50, notes that low tobacco prices at the end of the seventeenth century reduced the demand for slaves in the Chesapeake colonies and discouraged the Royal African Company from shipping even enough slaves to that area to meet the demand.

88. Berlin, *Many Thousands Gone*, 32.

89. Brugger, *Maryland*, 24.

90. "During the middle decades of the seventeenth century, there were places along the Bay where English colonials and Afro-Americans lived together as near equals." Menard, "Population, Economy, and Society," 86.

91. Berlin, *Generations of Captivity*, 62.

92. Berlin, *Many Thousands Gone*, 42.

93. Torrence, *Old Somerset*, 75–77, 491–92; Kimmel, "Free Blacks in Seventeenth Century Maryland," 22–25; Berlin, *Slaves without Masters*, 4–5.

94. Berlin, *Many Thousands Gone*, 33. Sometimes independent labor time was enlarged if slaves or servants undertook to feed and clothe themselves or if they shared some of their profits.

95. McConnell, "Black Experience in Maryland," 405. McConnell asserts that "the Johnsons became the first Negro family to settle on the Eastern Shore, if not the first in Maryland."

96. Kimmel, "Free Blacks in Seventeenth Century Maryland," 25.

97. Ibid.

98. Menard, "Population, Economy, and Society," 82.

99. Berlin, *Many Thousands Gone*, 29.

100. "Proceedings and Acts of the General Assembly January 1637/8-September 1664," *Archives MD* 1:533. Children born to slaves before 1664 served until they reached age thirty.

101. "Judging from the amount of debate time consumed and the large space devoted to them in the act, the vexing problems of miscegenation and the children born of such unions were the primary reasons for the 1664 Act." Johnson, "The Origin and Nature of African Slavery in Seventeenth Century Maryland," 238.

102. "Proceedings and Acts of the General Assembly January 1637/8-September 1664," *Archives MD* 1:534. Blackburn, *American Crucible*, 64, states that the English and Dutch were "urged by Puritan pastors to shun unions with 'strange women.'" Therefore, they developed "a more narrowly defined sense of religious and ethnic identity."

103. "Proceedings and Acts of the General Assembly January 1637/8–September 1664," *Archives MD* 1:534.

104. "Proceedings and Acts of the General Assembly, October 1678–November 1683," *Archives MD* 7:204.

105. That idea is seen again in 1692 when the Assembly said that marriage between a white woman and a black man (either slave or free) was "a disgrace not only of the English but also of many other Christian nations." The legislators went on to bind such white women as servants for seven years. The children of these liaisons were bound to age twenty-one if the couple was married and to age thirty-one if the child was a "bastard." "Proceedings and Acts of the General Assembly, April 1684–June 1692," *Archives MD* 13:546–49.

106. Kimmel, "Free Blacks in Seventeenth Century Maryland," 19, states that "the laws of the colonial period bearing upon blacks established an equation between blackness and slavery and thus implied that there was [*sic*] no such beings as free blacks."

107. "Proceedings and Acts of the General Assembly, April 1666–June 1676," *Archives MD* 2:523.

108. In the seventeenth century, racism was much less powerful and pervasive among whites than it would later become. Menard, "Population, Economy, and Society," 87.

109. Francis Johnson (grandson of Antonio), for example, signed a three-year indenture to George Phebus, a cooper in Somerset County, in order to learn a trade. Kimmel, "Free Blacks in Seventeenth Century Maryland," 25.

110. Berlin, *Generations of Captivity*, Table 1, 273.

111. Carr, Menard and Walsh, *Robert Cole's World*, 160. These authors calculate that blacks were 5 percent of Maryland's population in 1680.

112. Berlin, *Many Thousands Gone*, 8.

113. Menard, "Population, Economy, and Society," 86.

114. The act was to repeal one enacted on October 23, 1640. "Proceedings and Acts of the General Assembly, January 1637/8–September 1664," *Archives MD* 1:80, 496.

115. Brugger, *Maryland*, 98.

116. Menard, "Population, Economy, and Society," 88.

117. Brugger, *Maryland*, 46.

118. In 1671, the General Assembly passed an act eliminating the fear that some slave owners had that if their slaves were baptized they would be manumitted. "An Act for the Encourageing [*sic*] the Importacon [*sic*] of Negros [*sic*] and Slaves into this Province," *Archives MD* 2:272.

119. Between 1675 and 1695, about three thousand slaves were brought to the area. Berlin, *Many Thousands Gone*, 110.

120. From 1689 to 1715, Maryland was a royal colony. In 1715, King George I restored full proprietary rights to Benedict Leonard Calvert, the fourth Lord Baltimore, who had converted to Anglicanism.

121. "Proceedings and Acts of the General Assembly, September, 1704–April, 1706," *Archives MD* 26:636.

122. Clark, *Eastern Shore of Maryland and Virginia*, 259. The Eastern Shore's population was 20,376.

123. In southern Maryland, the two shores of the bay are quite close—Cove Point in Calvert County is less than ten miles west of Dorchester County.

124. Middleton, *Tobacco Coast*, 150.

125. Carr, Menard and Walsh, *Robert Cole's World*, 160.

126. Brugger, *Maryland*, 46.

127. "Prerogative Court (Wills)," *Archives MD*: Liber 1/folio 363, 9 December 1669/5 January 1669.

128. "Patent Records," *Archives MD* Liber 12/folio 92.

129. "Prerogative Court (Inventories)," *Archives MD* Liber 4/folio 273, November 17, 1720.

130. Middleton, *Tobacco Coast*, 151.

131. Berlin, *Generations of Captivity*, 45.

132. Middleton, *Tobacco Coast*, 155.

133. By 1750, Chestertown had replaced Oxford as the Eastern Shore's largest and most important town. Mullikin, *Old Line State*, 153.

134. Middleton, *Tobacco Coast*, 200.
135. In the eighteenth century, there was a spectacular rise in trade with the West Indies, with Maryland exporting wheat, corn, flour, pork and lumber. This stimulated shipbuilding and related industries such as the production of hemp, cordage, iron, sailcloth and naval stores. Middleton, *Tobacco Coast*, 175.
136. Brugger, *Maryland*, 78.
137. Beyond running advertisements, newspapers abetted the slave trade by acting as brokers and furnishing the venues for sales. Sublette and Sublette, *American Slave Coast*, 228.
138. Scharf, *History of Maryland*, 362.
139. "Proceedings and Acts of the General Assembly, October 1720–1723," *Archives MD* 34: 740ff. The act included the appointment of men in each county to carry out the law's provisions. Among those appointed for Dorchester County was Captain Henry Hooper.
140. Wright, *Cultural Life of the American Colonies*, 110.
141. Statistics for the graph taken from Berlin, *Generations of Captivity*, 273, Table 1: "Slave Population of the American Colonies and the United States, 1680–1860 (% of total population)."
142. Ibid.

Chapter 2: Two Revolutions

143. Population numbers for 1750 were 43,450 (31 percent). Berlin, Table 1: "Slave Population of the American Colonies and the United States, 1680–1860 (% of total population)," *Generations of Captivity*, 273.
144. Ibid., 54; Blackburn, *American Crucible*, 1, 6, 22. Blackburn defines the "plantation revolution" as a labor system with great intensification of slave work and slave subjection and with sharper racialization.
145. What distinguished the post-1670 Chesapeake was "the presence of a planter class able to command the region's resources, mobilize the power of the state, and vanquish competitors." Berlin, *Many Thousands Gone*, 10. See also 117 for how the planters linked themselves together.
146. By the 1710s, fewer than 10 percent of the planters worth £30 to £50 owned labor, and the majority of bound workers lived on estates appraised at more than £700. Menard, "Population, Economy, and Society," 88.
147. In Talbot County, only one planter had been worth £2,000 in 1680. In 1730, just one planter, Richard Bennett, was worth £20,000. Brugger,

Maryland, 59–60. See also Carr, Menard and Walsh, *Robert Cole's World*, 161. Small farmers were sometimes forced to become "clients of a planter patron." Non-slaveholding whites worked for the planters as hired help. Berlin, *Many Thousands Gone*, 96; Blackburn, *American Crucible*, 81.

148. Calculated from "Wealth at Death" as listed in Papenfuse, et al., "A Biographical Dictionary of the Maryland Legislature 1635–1789," *Archives MD* 426: 360, 361, 438, 457, 513, 537, 702 and 719.

149. Berlin, in *Slaves without Masters*, 85, quotes David Rice as writing to James Pemberton on January 16, 1790, "The rich hold Slaves, and the rich make the laws."

150. Blacks were thought to be "congenitally different." Berlin, *Many Thousands Gone*, 363. In 1790, Congressman William Loughton from South Carolina declared "that negroes were by nature an inferior race of beings." Quoted in Berlin, *Slaves without Masters*, 88.

151. Thomas Jefferson, *Notes on the State of Virginia*, ed. William Peden (Chapel Hill: University of North Carolina Press, 1954), 143, quoted in Berlin, *Long Emancipation*, 91.

152. Berlin, *Long Emancipation*, 65.

153. Ibid., 28. Per Berlin, "Malicious condescension."

154. Morison and Commager, *Growth of the American Republic*, 537.

155. Ibid., 539.

156. Franklin and Moss, *From Slavery to Freedom*, 189–90.

157. Berlin, *Many Thousands Gone*, 96.

158. *Maryland Gazette*, May 28, 1752. Benjamin Tasker Jr. (1720/21–1760) was surveyor general for the Eastern Shore from 1747 to 1755. Tasker's father was on the Governor's Council and briefly served as governor of Maryland (1753).

159. *Maryland Gazette*, July 15, 1760.

160. *Maryland Gazette*, September 29, 1767. They also advertised that they would take on tobacco for sale in London.

161. Wax, "Black Immigrants," 35; Berlin, *Many Thousands Gone*, 110, puts the figure from Senegambia and the Bight of Biafra (present-day Nigeria) at 75 percent.

162. Berlin, *Many Thousands Gone*, 115.

163. Middleton, *Tobacco Coast*, 154.

164. Wax, "Black Immigrants," 40.

165. Sublette and Sublette, *American Slave Coast*, 211.

166. Berlin, *Many Thousands Gone*, 5.

167. "The degradation of black life in mainland North America had many sources, but the largest was the growth of the plantation, a radically different form of social organization and commercial production controlled by a class of men whose appetite for labor was nearly insatiable." Berlin, *Generations of Captivity*, 54.

168. Berlin, *Many Thousands Gone*, 106, says that the phrase "'to work like a slave' took on a profound and chilling meaning for all working people." For an example of the treatment of slaves on the Eastern Shore, see Douglass, *My Bondage and My Freedom*, 178–89.

169. Menard, "Population, Economy, and Society," 82.

170. Berlin, *Many Thousands Gone*, 113, 118. Quotation from Berlin, *Making of African America*, 54.

171. Berlin, *Many Thousands Gone*, 116–17; Carr, Menard and Walsh, *Robert Cole's World*, 70. Quotation in Brugger, *Maryland*, 238.

172. Berlin, *Many Thousands Gone*, 115. Conditions were even worse for women. See Jacobs, *Incidents in the Life of a Slave Girl*, online at docsouth.unc.edu/fpn/jacobs.html.

173. Berlin, *Many Thousands Gone*, 98, calls the violence on the plantation "systematic and relentless."

174. Douglass, *My Bondage and My Freedom*, 201–2.

175. Berlin, *Generations of Captivity*, 56.

176. Douglass, *My Bondage and My Freedom*, 142. Berlin, *Generations of Captivity*, 58, states that planters stripped away all family ties because the enslaved person's identity rested upon family connections, and planters wanted their slaves to be totally dependent upon their owners.

177. Blackburn, *American Crucible*, 78; Berlin, *Making of African America*, 85.

178. Blackburn, *American Crucible*, 64; Berlin, *Generations of Captivity*, 64.

179. Berlin, *Many Thousands Gone*, 96.

180. An English prelate wrote in 1680: "These two words, *Negro* and Slave" had "by custom grown Homogeneous and convertible." In Morgan Godwyn, *The Negro's and Indians Advocate* (London, 1680), 36, quoted in Berlin, *Many Thousands Gone*, 97, 123. Berlin further notes that tobacco planters "collapsed all black people, free and slave, into one subaltern class, in which color—not nationality, skill, or religion—defined all."

181. Morgan, *American Slavery, American Freedom*, 386.

182. Sublette and Sublette, *American Slave Coast*, 87, state that the idea of separating blacks from whites went back as far as the reign of Elizabeth I. The queen called black people "Negars and

Blackamoors" and tried to remove them from England because they were "Infidels."

183. Berlin, *Generations of Captivity*, 2.

184. Ibid., 62.

185. William Green, *Narrative of Events in the Life of William Green (Formerly a Slave), Written by Himself* (Philadelphia: Rhistoric Press, 1969 [Springfield MA, 1853]), 7–8, quoted in Brugger, *Maryland*, 236.

186. "In the slave colonies there was no one who could restrain the planter." Blackburn, *American Crucible*, 93.

187. Land, "Colonial Period," 22; Berlin, *Many Thousands Gone*, 97–98.

188. Douglass, *Narrative of the Life*, 68–69. He cites Reverend Daniel Weeden and Reverend Rigby Hopkins of the Reformed Methodist Church in St. Michaels, Maryland, as examples.

189. Berlin, *Many Thousands Gone*, 3, notes that owners "presumed their own absolute sovereignty," but "slaves never relinquished the right to control their own destiny."

190. Quarles, "'Freedom Fettered,'" 301; Berlin, *Many Thousands Gone*, 11, 133.

191. Smith, "Minty's Legacy," 9; Douglass, *My Bondage and My Freedom*, 142.

192. Berlin, *Generations of Captivity*, 57, notes that removing African names took away "the lineage that structured much of African life."

193. Ibid., 39.

194. Douglass, *My Bondage and My Freedom*, 164; Berlin, *Slaves without Masters*, 52.

195. Berlin, *Many Thousands Gone*, 112, quotes Virginia slaveholder Robert "King" Carter: "I nam'd them here & by their names we can always know what sizes they are of & I am sure we repeated them so often to them that every one knew their names & would readily answer to them." His overseers were careful to see that the slaves "always go by the names we gave them."

196. Berlin, *Many Thousands Gone*, 95.

197. Patuson Tom is identified in the will of Matthew Travers (1742). "Prerogative Court (Wills)," *Archives MD*: Liber 22/folio 502. Harry Boy is named in the will of Henry Hooper (1720). "Prerogative Court (Wills)," *Archives MD*: Liber 16/folio 159.

198. Douglass, *Narrative of the Life*, 15.

199. Berlin, *Long Emancipation*, 73.

200. Douglass, *My Bondage and My Freedom*, 140.

201. Ibid. Douglass wrote, "My father was a white man…but of the correctness of this opinion [that Aaron Anthony was his father], I know

nothing; the means of knowing was withheld from me" (140). "Slavery does away with fathers, as it does away with families" (151).

202. Ibid., 149.

203. Franklin and Moss, *From Slavery to Freedom*, 125. Laws were framed so as not to deprive the owner of the slave's labor for long, so whipping, branding and short terms of imprisonment were the norm. Arson, rape of a white woman and conspiracy to rebel were capital offenses in all the slave states.

204. "Acts of the General Assembly hitherto unpublished 1694–1698, 1711–1729," *Archives MD* 38:48–49.

205. "An Abridgement of the Laws in Force and Use in Her Majesty's Plantations; 1704," *Archives MD* 193:68.

206. Slave owners thought runaways would try to pass for Indians. See the *Maryland Gazette*, May 21, 1752, advertisement where Henry Waggaman of Somerset County said of his runaway, he "looks very much like an *Indian*, and will endeavour to pass for such when it suits him." *Archives MD* MSA SC2731.

207. "Proceedings and Acts of the General Assembly, 1727–1729 with Appendix of Statutes, 1714–1726," *Archives MD* 36:583–86.

208. Ibid., 36:454–55.

209. "Proceedings and Acts of the General Assembly, 1737–1740," *Archives MD* 40:92–95.

210. "Proceedings and Acts of the General Assembly, 1752–1754," *Archives MD* 50:76–78.

211. *Dorchester County Court, Land Records (1669–)* [hereafter *DCLR*] MSA CE 46-10, 9 Old 459/21 May 1737.

212. Sublette and Sublette, *American Slave Coast*, 40.

213. *DCLR*, MSA CE 46-53, 2 ER 291/2 January 1813.

214. "Prerogative Court (Wills)," *Archives MD*: Liber 22/folio 248.

215. Berlin, *Generations of Captivity*, 115.

216. Berlin, *Many Thousands Gone*, 131.

217. Middleton, *Tobacco Coast*, 199–200, notes that tobacco production on the Eastern Shore had been declining since the end of the seventeenth century. Menard states that beginning in the 1740s, rising demand for food in Europe and the West Indies created new opportunities for Chesapeake planters. Menard, "Population, Economy, and Society," 79; Brugger, *Maryland*, 64; Berlin, *Many Thousands Gone*, 134–35, 268.

218. Brugger, *Maryland*, 65; Berlin, *Many Thousands Gone*, 134; Mullikin, "Eastern Shore," 154.

219. Middleton, *Tobacco Coast*, 199, 245, 251. Brugger, *Maryland*, 64, mentions shipyards at Third Haven and Island Creek in Talbot County, at Chestertown in Kent County and at West River near Annapolis.

220. Middleton, *Tobacco Coast*, 199–200.

221. Wax, "Black Immigrants," 37; Bast, "Benjamin Keene, 1694–1770," 51.

222. Berlin, *Slaves without Masters*, 63.

223. Slaves became carpenters, coopers, boatmen, cooks, wagoners, warehouse keepers and wharfingers. Berlin, *Many Thousands Gone*, 135–36, 269, 276.

224. Berlin, *Generations of Captivity*, 114, 221–23. "Hiring—as much as any other feature of slavery—distinguished black life in the Upper South from the plantation interior" (223). When slaves could hire themselves out, there were greater opportunities to save some cash. Berlin, *Slaves without Masters*, 35.

225. Berlin, *Many Thousands Gone*, 275. Slave-hiring contracts were usually for one year, beginning on January 2 and ending on Christmas Eve. Sublette and Sublette, *American Slave Coast*, 584–85, 588. The authors note that the "great peril" of being hired out was that those who hired often cared little for the well-being of the slaves they hired.

226. Mullikin, "Eastern Shore," 155–56, states that the semi-isolation of the Eastern Shore increased with the passage of time rather than diminished and that by the early 1800s "the vast majority of Shoremen never set foot off their native peninsula."

227. The Eastern Shore "developed a flavor all its own." Brugger, *Maryland*, 159.

228. Mullikin, "Eastern Shore," 156. In chapter 1 of *The Road to Jim Crow*, C. Christopher Brown describes the Eastern Shore as "A Land Apart."

229. Berlin, *Generations of Captivity*, 114.

230. Berlin, *Making of African America*, 105.

231. Carroll, *Three Hundred Years and More*, 14. Carroll uses the term "community" rather than "brotherhood."

232. George Fox, quoted in Bordewich, *Bound for Canaan*, 53.

233. Brugger, *Maryland*, 29. Carroll, *Three Hundred Years and More*, 25, identifies the four meetings as Bayside, Betty's Cove, Choptank and Tuckahoe. Third Haven replaced Betty's Cove in 1693.

234. *Old Third Haven Meeting House 1684* (405 S. Washington Street, Easton, Maryland 21601), church brochure.

235. Torrence, *Old Somerset*, 12. The Virginia Assembly referred to Quakers as "an unreasonable and turbulent sort of people who daily gather together

unlawful assemblies of people, teaching lies, miracles, false visions, prophecies, and doctrines tending to disturb the peace, disorganize society and destroy all law and government and religion."

236. Brugger, *Maryland*, 29. Torrence, *Old Somerset*, 9, notes that having organized settlements along the Maryland/Virginia border would help to secure Lord Baltimore's charter rights there. The Quakers established the "hundreds" of Manokin and Annemessex in Somerset County.

237. Carroll, *Three Hundred Years and More*, 37; Carroll, "Berry Brothers," 1. Carroll suggests that no Quakers spoke against slavery until after Fox's visit.

238. Carroll, *Three Hundred Years and More*, 38.

239. Brugger, *Maryland*, 167. See also Carroll, "Berry Brothers," 2.

240. Woolman wrote essays about slavery, including "Some Considerations on the Keeping of Negroes" in 1754 and a second version of that essay in 1772. Carroll, *Three Hundred Years and More*, 39. Woolman's quotation from Blackburn, *American Crucible*, 157.

241. Carroll, "Berry Brothers," 4. James, Joseph and Benjamin Berry all freed slaves between 1767 and 1769, as did their sister-in-law Sarah Powell.

242. Talbot County Court, Land Records (1662–), MSA CE 90-21, 19 JL 496/26 April 1768.

243. Ibid., 19 JL 499/17 May 1768.

244. *DCLR*, MSA CE 46-23, 22 Old 308 & 309/8 April 1768.

245. In Maryland, Daniel Dulaney Jr. wrote an unsigned essay in which he argued that only the General Assembly could tax Marylanders. See Brugger, *Maryland*, 104–6.

246. Ibid., 107.

247. Ibid., 113. Maryland sent Samuel Chase, Thomas Johnson and William Paca from the western shore and Matthew Tilghman and Robert Goldsborough from the Eastern Shore.

248. Crowl, "Revolution and After: 1774–1789," 37. The burning took place on October 14, 1774. Brugger, *Maryland*, 113.

249. Calderhead, "Thomas Carney," 319.

250. Ibid.

251. Berlin, *Slaves without Masters*, 18.

252. McConnell, "Black Experience in Maryland," 406; Berlin, *Many Thousands Gone*, 260.

253. Berlin, *Slaves without Masters*, 19, suggests that black recruits were given a shovel more often than a musket.

254. Calderhead, "Thomas Carney," 319–26.
255. Berlin, *Slaves without Masters*, 17–18. Berlin says the number of escapees was perhaps eight hundred, "and more important, hundreds more heard of his promise of freedom and were infected with the dream of liberty." It was so easy for slaves who lived on plantations along the water to flee that in 1781 the Council urged the General Assembly to pass special legislation to protect slave property.
256. Sublette and Sublette, *American Slave Coast*, 255–57.
257. Brugger, *Maryland*, 123, notes that "white folk" on the Eastern Shore were frightened by Dunmore's raids.
258. Berlin, *Many Thousands Gone*, 257–58.
259. Berlin, *Generations of Captivity*, 112.
260. Brugger, *Maryland*, 123; Berlin, *Many Thousands Gone*, 258.
261. Ronald Hoffman, *A Spirit of Dissension: Economics, Politics, and the Revolution in Maryland* (Baltimore, MD: Johns Hopkins University Press, 1973), 147–48, quoted in Berlin, *Many Thousands Gone*, 261. The local Committee of Safety collected eight guns, along with swords and bayonets.
262. Berlin, *Many Thousands Gone*, 259.
263. When the British evacuated Yorktown, they took hundreds of slaves with them. When they evacuated New York in 1783, they took over one thousand Virginia and Maryland slaves to freedom. Berlin, *Many Thousands Gone*, 263, asserts that more than five thousand slaves from the Upper South escaped during the Revolutionary War.
264. Sublette and Sublette, *American Slave Coast*, 283.
265. Quotation from Philip Foner, ed., *The Complete Writings of Thomas Paine*, 2 vols. (New York: Citadel Press, 1945), 2:15–19, in Berlin, *Many Thousands Gone*, 220.
266. Berlin, *Slaves without Masters*, 20, 21, 24. Abolitionists talked about the negative effect of slavery on white society, claiming that slavery "threatened to subvert the moral foundations of the new Republic" (24).
267. Bordewich, *Bound for Canaan*, 32, quoted in Thomas, *Slave Trade*, 500.
268. Berlin, *Long Emancipation*, 61.
269. Blackburn, *American Crucible*, 161; Berlin, *Many Thousands Gone*, 232.
270. Sublette and Sublette, *American Slave Coast*, 286, notes that once the Constitution was adopted, the Northwest Ordinance "no longer had legal force." It did seem, however, to discourage slaveholders from moving to the area. Blackburn, *American Crucible*, 332, states that the Northwest Ordinance of 1784 and the end of the African slave trade in 1808 "did imply that there was something wrong with slavery."

271. Berlin, *Slaves without Masters*, 21.
272. Brugger, *Maryland*, 169; Thomas Herty, "A Digest of the Laws of Maryland," *Archives MD:* MSA SC M 3150, 353.
273. "Proceedings and Acts of the General Assembly, 1796," *Archives MD* 105:249ff. "An ACT relating to negroes" (Laws of Maryland, 1796, Chapt. LXVII) was a lengthy act relating to manumission, the transit of slaves in and out of the state, fraudulent exports of free blacks and slaves with terms to serve, etc. It also repealed a number of previous acts passed by the Assembly.
274. Berlin, *Slaves without Masters*, 35.
275. Ibid., 30.
276. *DCLR*, MSA CE 46-34, 2 HD 550/20 February 1790.
277. *DCLR*, MSA CE 46-34, 2 HD 558/17 March 1790.
278. *DCLR*, MSA CE 46-34, 2 HD 681/1 June 1790.
279. *DCLR*, MSA CE 46-41, 14 HD 312/23 July 1798. Deed of manumission accessed from https:/mdlandrec.net.
280. Quarles, "'Freedom Fettered,'" 303.
281. Berlin, *Slaves without Masters*, 91.
282. Ibid., 33. Berlin quotes one Maryland abolitionist as saying, "Whole families were often liberated by a single verdict, the fate of one relative deciding the fate of many."
283. The Butler case can be traced online at the Maryland Archives "Legacy of Slavery" site at http://msa.maryland.gov/megfile/msa/speccol/sc5400/sc5496/000500/000534/html/00534bio.html.
284. "Proceedings and Acts of the General Assembly, October 1678–November 1683," *Archives MD* 7:204. This act released from slavery white servant women who had married black men and their mulatto children if the marriage was encouraged by their master.
285. Heinegg, *Free African Americans*, 2.
286. Brugger, *Maryland*, 169.
287. As many as 120 to 300 other local slaves could trace their status back to Eleanor Butler. Walsh, "Rural African Americans," 335.
288. Helen T. Catterall, ed., *Judicial Cases Concerning Slavery and the Negro*, vol. 4, 54, quoted in Berlin, *Slaves without Masters*, 34.
289. Berlin, *Slaves without Masters*, 24–5.
290. Brugger, *Maryland*, 167.
291. Carroll, *Three Hundred Years and More*, 41.
292. Ibid.
293. Brugger, *Maryland*, 167.

294. Berlin, *Many Thousands Gone*, 138–39, 220; Brugger, *Maryland*, 167. Believing that all men were equal in God's sight, they accepted black and white converts "with equal enthusiasm."
295. McConnell, "Black Experience in Maryland," 406.
296. *DCLR*, MSA CE 46-33, 9 NH 348/30 August 1787.
297. *DCLR*, MSA CE 46-34, 2 HD 558/25 March 1790.
298. *DCLR*, MSA CE 46-33, 9 NH 348/30 August 1787.
299. *DCLR*, MSA CE 46-34, 2 HD 558/25 March 1790.
300. Berlin, *Many Thousands Gone*, 279.
301. *DCLR*, MSA CE 46-50, 25 HD 198/23 July 1808.
302. *DCLR*, MSA CE 46-59, 9 ER 296/17 February 1824.
303. Berlin, *Many Thousands Gone*, 280.
304. As late as 1818, the General Assembly of the Presbyterian Church had spoken against slavery as "inconsistent with the law of God." But, like the Methodists, they changed that position. Bordewich, *Bound for Canaan*, 87; Berlin, *Slaves without Masters*, 84.
305. Even though the Methodist Church encouraged black preachers and wrote antislavery principles into its bylaws, "many Methodists shared the racist assumptions of Negro inferiority and subordination." Berlin, *Slaves without Masters*, 71.
306. Ibid., 83.
307. The Southern Baptist Convention supported the Confederacy during the Civil War and "provided the biblical justifications for slavery." They propagated "the mythology of the Lost Cause: the cult of fallen heroes and the idealization of anti-bellum white culture as chivalrous, decent, and pure." To Southern Baptists, "the South was the most spiritual part of the country, the only one to hold to the truth of the New Testament Gospels, a sacred soil and the saving remnant of pure Anglo-Saxon culture." Fitzgerald, *Evangelicals*, 225.
308. Ibid., 51, 52.
309. The word *slave* is seldom used in the Bible. More often, the word *servant* is used: Ephesians 6:5, Colossians 3:22, Titus 2:9 and Peter 2:18. Servants are admonished to be obedient to their masters and please them in all things.
310. Berlin, *Slaves without Masters*, 79.

Chapter 3: "Selling South"

311. Wright, *Free Negro in Maryland*, 23; Berlin, *Many Thousands Gone*, 283.

312. "Table 2: Free Negro Population, 1755–1810," "Table 3: Percent Increase of Free Negroes, 1755–1810" and "Table 4: Proportion of Negroes Free, 1755–1810," Berlin, *Slaves without Masters*, 46–47.

313. Ibid., 3.

314. Ibid., 46. Berlin calculates that increase of free blacks in Maryland from 1755 to 1790 was 342.7 percent.

315. Total black population in 1790 was 111,079. See "Table 2. Free Black Population of the United States, 1790–1820," Berlin, *Generations of Captivity*, 276–77.

316. Graph statistics are taken from Clark, *Eastern Shore of Maryland and Virginia*, 511. Talbot County had 1,076 free blacks in 1790; Worcester County had 1,059 in 1810.

317. Wright, *Free Negro in Maryland*, 318, says that outside Baltimore, freemen and slaves "were not widely different from each other." Heinegg, in his introduction to *Free African Americans of Maryland and Delaware*, states that African Americans in Maryland in the colonial period had closer relations with the local slave population than did their counterparts in Delaware, Virginia and North Carolina. Berlin, *Many Thousands Gone*, 289, asserts that black society was "much more of one piece" in the Upper South than in the North.

318. Berlin, *Generations of Captivity*, 120.

319. Berlin, *Slaves without Masters*, 10. "Negroes banded together not to enjoy a common linguistic, cultural and religious tradition, but because a systematic pattern of discrimination left them no alternative." Quoted in Berlin, *Making of African America*, 38.

320. Berlin, *Slaves without Masters*, 69.

321. Ibid., 63.

322. Wright, *Free Negro in Maryland*, 184.

323. In 1830, approximately 2 percent of Maryland's slave population was owned by "persons of color." Bridner, "Fugitive Slaves of Maryland," 34.

324. *DCLR*, MSA CE46-53, 2 ER 296; MSA CE46-55, 4 ER 239/14 September 1816; MSA CE46-56, 5 ER 465/3 March 1819.

325. Berlin, *Generations of Captivity*, 232. The flexibility in white attitudes of the colonial era disappeared when the number of free blacks increased enough to be deemed a threat to white control. See Berlin, *Slaves without Masters*, xiii–xiv, 7, 9, 90.

326. "Throughout the South, free Negroes found their mobility curbed, their economic opportunities limited, and their civil rights all but obliterated." Berlin, *Slaves without Masters*, 90.

327. "By 1800…Maryland committed itself more explicitly than ever before to slavery and to a subordinate role for the free black." Quarles, "'Freedom Fettered,'" 302. "Place" for blacks meant the necessity to tip one's hat to the white man on the street, to look down, to vacate the sidewalk. Berlin, *Slaves without Masters*, 182.

328. Quarles, "'Freedom Fettered,'" 302.

329. "Proceedings and Acts of the General Assembly, 1796," *Archives MD* 105: 249ff.

330. "Session Laws, 1801, Chapter XC," *Archives MD* 558:87.

331. Brugger, *Maryland*, 171.

332. "Session Laws, 1805, Chapter LXVI" (passed January 15, 1806), *Archives MD* 607:46; Berlin, *Slaves without Masters*, 93.

333. "Session Laws, 1806, Chapter LXXXI" (passed January 4, 1807), *Archives MD* 608:46.

334. "Session Laws, 1805, Chapter LXXX" (passed January 25, 1806), *Archives MD* 607:60.

335. Berlin, *Slaves without Masters*, 92.

336. Ibid., 187. Berlin, *Long Emancipation*, 110, asserts that white northerners "eroded their own moral authority respecting slavery" when they continually proscribed the lives of their free black populations.

337. Letter to E.B. Caldwell, secretary of the American Colonization Society, 1818, quoted in Berlin, *Slaves without Masters*, 187–88.

338. Berlin, *Generations of Captivity*, 273. Table 1, 32 percent of the population.

339. Ibid. Larger numbers, but still about one-third of the total population.

340. Berlin, *Many Thousands Gone*, 264.

341. Letter, "Thomas Jefferson to John Wayles Eppes, June 30, 1820," Founders Online, National Archives, last modified June 29, 2017, http://founders.archive.gov/documents/Jefferson/98-01-02-1352.

342. Letter from Charles Carroll of Annapolis to son Charles Carroll of Carrollton, December 3, 1773, quoted in Sublette and Sublette, *American Slave Coast*, 204–5.

343. Douglass, *My Bondage and My Freedom*, 267.

344. Ibid.

345. Between 1775 and 1783, an additional forty-seven babies were born in the slave quarter of Henry Holliday's Talbot County plantation. That far

surpassed the increase from 1749 to 1774 when, on average, two babies a year were born. Walsh, "Rural African Americans," 332.

346. Berlin, *Many Thousands Gone*, 267.

347. U.S. Constitution, Article I, Section 9. Sublette and Sublette, *American Slave Coast*, 15, suggests that Jefferson, in asking for this law, was not acting for humanitarian reasons. Rather, he was assuring that the price of "domestically raised people" would remain high.

348. Schomburg Center for Research in Black Culture, "The Act of 1807," http://abolition.nypl.org/content/docs/text/Act_of_1807.pdf.

349. Ibid.

350. Berlin, *Making of African America*, 99.

351. "An ACT to prohibit the bringing slaves in to this state," in "Hanson's Laws of Maryland 1763–1784," *Archives MD* 203:350.

352. Skyrocketing prices for slaves after 1808 tempted adventurers to run the blockade. Thomas, *Slave Trade*, 519; Berlin, *Generations of Captivity*, 167.

353. Author's visit to the Pompey Slave Museum in Nassau, New Providence Island, Bahamas, on January 20, 2017. Lloyd's is an insurance market that was founded in 1686 by Edward Lloyd at his coffee house on Tower Street in the city of London. Many sea captains and sailors frequented his establishment, and Lloyd first created a system to provide marine insurance. The company insured many slavers. Archaeologists recovered the remains of the *Peter Mowell* in 2012.

354. Thomas, *Slave Trade*, 616.

355. Berlin, *Many Thousands Gone*, 264.

356. Berlin, *Generations of Captivity*, 161, calls the second Middle Passage "the central event in the lives of African-American people between the American Revolution and slavery's demise in December 1865."

357. Ibid., 213.

358. Ibid., 126, 213.

359. Berlin, *Many Thousands Gone*, 265.

360. Neimeyer, *War in the Chesapeake*, 68.

361. Ibid., 78–79, 104–6.

362. Mullikin, "Eastern Shore," 156.

363. Neimeyer, *War in the Chesapeake*, 79, 117, 145; quotation 120. See also George, "Mirage of Freedom," 40.

364. "Daniel Wright," *Archives of Maryland* (Biographical Series), MSA SC 5496-51069, accessed at www.msa.maryland.gov.

365. George, "Mirage of Freedom," 43.

366. Cochrane had written to the governor of Canada: "It is my intention to fortify one of the Islands in the Chesapeake to facilitate the desertion of the Negroes, and their Families, who are to have their choice of either entering into His Majesty's Service, or to be Settled with their Families at Trinidad or in the British American Provinces." Vice Admiral Sir Alexander Cochrane to Governor-General Sir George Prevost, March 11, 1814, in *The Naval War of 1812: A Documentary History*, ed. Michael J. Crawford (Washington, D.C.: Naval Historical Center, 2002), 38–40, cited in Neimeyer, *War in the Chesapeake*, 117.

367. Neimeyer, *War in the Chesapeake*, 119–21. Neimeyer asserts that at least 19 percent of runaway male slaves became Colonial Marines—what he calls "a fairly high percentage." The Colonial Marines with Cockburn included Mentor "Manto" Beauchamp from Somerset County; John Chambers, Abraham Lyles, Elijah Lyles and George Horner from Kent County; and Tom Johnson from Talbot County. Their stories are available online at "Slavery & the War of 1812," Legacy of Slavery in Maryland, accessed at www.msa.maryland.gov.

368. Value was $1,204,960. Sublette and Sublette, *American Slave Coast*, 403.

369. Berlin, *Many Thousands Gone*, 14.

370. Bridner, "Fugitive Slaves of Maryland," 47.

371. Berlin, *Generations of Captivity*, 167. "Manstealing" became so common that people complained to Congress. Berlin, *Slaves without Masters*, 99, 160.

372. The gang usually included Ebenezer Johnson, Thomas Collins, John Purnell and Cyrus James. Morgan, *Delmarva's Patty Cannon*, 36, 48.

373. According to the *Delaware Gazette and American Watchman*, April 17, 1829, Patty "resembled a man more than a woman." Quoted in Miller, "Patty Cannon," 421.

374. Morgan, *Delmarva's Patty Cannon*, 36.

375. The loss of free blacks would be ignored by Eastern Shore slave owners. Miller, "Patty Cannon," 419; Berlin, *Making of African America*, 102.

376. Townsend, *Entailed Hat*, ix.

377. Patty Cannon died on May 11, 1829. Miller, "Patty Cannon," 423.

378. Kidnapping became "a growth industry." Berlin, *Long Emancipation*, 134, 137. Kidnappers were known as "blackbirders."

379. Berlin, *Slaves without Masters*, 104; Bordewich, *America's Great Debate*, 174, notes that the vast majority of those opposed to slavery "were personally uncomfortable around blacks."

380. Berlin, *Many Thousands Gone*, 227.

381. The founders believed that freed slaves should be returned to Africa, Christianized and "prepared to redeem Africa from barbarism and idolatry." Bordewich, *America's Great Debate*, 94.

382. Berlin, *Slaves without Masters*, 48, 207, 213. Not all Maryland whites supported the colonization idea. Many tidewater farmers with small acreage and too little money to afford slaves opposed colonization because it would "make laboring men scarce" (207).

383. Bordewich, *Bound for Canaan*, 161.

384. "Session Laws, 1831," *Archives MD* 213:45ff, chapter 323.

385. A lengthy description of the Maryland colonization project can be read online at slavery.msa.maryland.gov/html/casestudies/mscs_overview.pdf.

386. By 1837, the settlement had more than two hundred people. Brugger, *Maryland*, 213.

387. "Session Laws, 1831," *Archives MD* 213:343. In 1852, the Maryland legislature renewed support of colonization for another five years. Berlin, *Slaves without Masters*, 355.

388. Thomas Fuller, *Maryland Colonization Journal* 8, no. 7 (December 1855), quoted in Brown, *Road to Jim Crow*, 95.

389. "Luke Walker," *Archives MD* (Biographical Series), MSA SC 5496-5120, msa.maryland.gov.

390. "Eben Parker," *Archives MD* (Biographical Series), MSA SC 5496-5135, msa.maryland.gov.

391. Brown, *Road to Jim Crow*, 93.

392. The net result was 627 immigrants to Africa and 25 to Haiti at a cost of over $66,000. McConnell, "Black Experience in Maryland," 411. Free blacks strongly resisted the state's efforts to expatriate them.

393. The second Middle Passage relocated almost double the number of Africans carried to mainland North America in the first passage. Berlin, *Many Thousands Gone*, 359.

394. The phrase is taken from Ball, "Slavery's Trail of Tears," 59.

395. Berlin, *Many Thousands Gone*, 135, 267.

396. Ibid., 265. Sometimes slave sales also gave farmers the funds necessary to finance the next growing season. See Berlin, *Making of African America*, 106.

397. Sublette and Sublette, *American Slave Coast*, 40. Berlin, *Generations of Captivity*, 113, estimates that 115,000 slaves left the tidewater region between 1780 and 1810 in what was called the "Georgia trade."

398. Talbot County Court (Land Records) 1818–1819, MSA CE 90-44, j1 41/01-2, accessible at https://mdlandrec.net.

NOTES TO PAGES 82–90

399. Ibid., jl 41/02-4.
400. Ibid., jl 41/04-5. According to www.westegg.com/inflation (inflation calculator), that would be equivalent to $36,322.12 today.
401. When Georgia and the Carolinas had relinquished their claims to territory to the west of them, they had stipulated that any new states in the area should be slaveholding.
402. Sublette and Sublette, American Slave Coast, 469.
403. Today, the property houses the Urban League of Northern Virginia and its Freedom House.
404. Sullivan, "Healing a Painful Past," C6.
405. Douglass, "Internal Slave Trade: Extract from an Oration, at Rochester, July 5, 1852," Autobiographies, 437.
406. Coffles usually contained fifty or sixty slaves, at most one hundred. Sublette and Sublette, American Slave Coast, 475.
407. Berlin, Making of African America, 112.
408. Ibid., 116.
409. Ball, Fifty Years in Chains, 29–30.
410. Sublette and Sublette, American Slave Coast, 6.
411. Douglass, Narrative of the Life, 24.
412. Sublette and Sublette, American Slave Coast, 8–9.
413. Ibid., 407. Baltimore, Alexandria, Washington, Norfolk and Richmond were the major northern terminals of the trade and Natchez, New Orleans and Vicksburg the southern ones.
414. Berlin, Making of African America, 113–14.
415. Ibid., 102.
416. Sublette and Sublette, American Slave Coast, 433, says that Woolfolk was like a "bogeyman" for slave children.
417. Ibid., 429.
418. Berlin, Making of African America, 103.
419. Sublette and Sublette, American Slave Coast, 433.
420. Clayton, "Baltimore's Own Version of Amistad.'"
421. Schermerhorn, "'What Else You Should Know.'"
422. Ibid.
423. Berlin, Slaves without Masters, 209.
424. 1930 United States Federal Census, District 6 (Dorchester, Maryland), digital images Ancestry.com [database online] from National Archives microrepublication M19, roll 56, 252–54; 1840 United States Federal Census, District 6 (Dorchester, Maryland), digital images Ancestry.com [database online] from National Archives microrepublication M704, roll 165, 102–03.

Whites numbered 324 in 1830, 357 in 1840. Slaves numbered 69 in 1830, 43 in 1840. Free blacks numbered 50 in 1830, 63 in 1840.

425. In Dorchester County, the drop was from 5,001 to 4,227—a 15.5 percent drop.

426. Berlin, *Making of African America*, 80.

427. In fact, "veterans of the plantation business advised 'it is better to buy *none in families*, but to *select only choice, first rate, young hands from 14 to 25 years of age* (buying no children or aged negroes).'" Steven F. Miller, "Plantation Labor Organization and Slave Life on the Cotton Frontier: The Alabama-Mississippi Black Belt, 1815–1840," quoted in Berlin, *Generations of Captivity*, 169.

428. Berlin, *Making of African America*, 110.

429. The number of runaways had increased significantly during the years of the Revolutionary War, and that increase continued after the war was over. Berlin, *Slaves without Masters*, 36, 157.

430. Larson, *Bound for the Promised Land*, 2.

431. Fugitive slave advertisement for Nellie Keene placed by Levin Woolford, *Easton Gazette*, April 12, 1831.

432. Fugitive slave advertisement for Bob, Jake and George placed by John Simmons and Jacob Pattison, *American and Commercial Daily Advertiser*, October 15, 1836.

433. Fugitive slave advertisement for Lewis and John and Emory Drake placed by Edward P. Gollorthon, *American and Commercial Daily Advertiser*, July 2, 1842.

434. Berlin, *Slaves without Masters*, 41, 159.

435. Nix and Hess, "Preserving the Warden House," 17.

436. Douglass, *Narrative of the Life*, 20.

437. For a description of the Lloyd estate at Wye see Douglass, "Survey of the Slave Plantation" and "Life in the Great House," *My Bondage and My Freedom*, 158–70 and 190–98.

438. Papenfuse, et al., "A Biographical Dictionary of the Maryland Legislature 1631–1789," *Archives MD* 426:539.

439. A lengthy description of the abuse Douglass suffered at the hands of Aunt Katy can be found in Douglass, *My Bondage and My Freedom*, 153–54.

440. Ibid., 207. Douglass wrote, "Miss Lucretia was my friend."

441. Quotation from Douglass, *Narrative of the Life*, 26; Douglass, *My Bondage and My Freedom*, 194–95.

442. Douglass, *My Bondage and My Freedom*, 212.

443. Douglass, *Narrative of the Life*, 36–38, 41.

444. Ibid., 41–42.

445. Ibid., 44–45.

446. Ibid., 49.

447. Douglass, *My Bondage and My Freedom*, 246. When Douglass was sent to work for Edward Covey, he went there with the anticipation that he would be getting enough to eat.

448. Douglass, *Narrative of the Life*, 54.

449. Douglass, *My Bondage and My Freedom*, 264.

450. Ibid., 187–88.

451. Ibid., 260.

452. Douglass, *Narrative of the Life*, 58.

453. Ibid., 21.

454. Douglass, *My Bondage and My Freedom*, 325, 336.

455. Douglass, *Life and Times*, 642–47.

456. Douglass, *Narrative of the Life*, 91–93.

457. Ibid., 95.

Chapter 4: Abolition, the Fugitive Slave Act and the Underground Railroad

458. The earliest abolition society was established by Quakers in Pennsylvania in 1774. Two members of that organization were from the Eastern Shore of Maryland—John Needles of Talbot County and Joseph Wilkinson of Kent County. Carroll, "Voices of Protest," 350.

459. "Votes and Proceedings of the Senate of the State of Maryland," *Archives MD* MSA SC M 3185, 993.

460. "Votes and Proceedings of the House of Delegates of the State of Maryland," *Archives MD* MSA SC M 3197, 1041. See also Brugger, *Maryland*, 168.

461. McConnell, "Black Experience in Maryland," 406.

462. Carroll, "Voices of Protest," 351–52.

463. McConnell, "Black Experience in Maryland," 406.

464. Berlin, *Slaves without Masters*, 81. The House of Delegates by a vote of fifty to thirteen called a memorial by the society "indecent, illiberal, highly reprehensible, and, moreover, as untrue as it is illiberal." "Votes and Proceedings of the House of Delegates of the State of Maryland," *Archives MD*, MSA SCM 3197, 1316.

465. Berlin, *Slaves without Masters*, 84.
466. Statistics taken from Thomas, *Slave Trade*, 571.
467. Sublette and Sublette, *American Slave Coast*, 331. Watt's steam engine enabled entrepreneurs to build textile mills in locations that did not have access to water power.
468. Blackburn, *American Crucible*, 24.
469. Franklin and Moss, *From Slavery to Freedom*, 173–74.
470. There were many female abolitionists because they saw the similarity of slavery to their own condition, as a married woman was considered her husband's property. Sublette and Sublette, *American Slave Coast*, 377.
471. Brugger, *Maryland*, 215.
472. Ibid.
473. Douglass, *Narrative of the Life*, 43.
474. Berlin, *Long Emancipation*, 130.
475. Quoted in Sublette and Sublette, *American Slave Coast*, 425.
476. Britain freed 750,000 slaves. The compensation package totaled £20 million, which today would be over $2.4 billion. Compensation conversion from Nye, "Pounds Sterling to Dollars," accessed at http://www.uwyo.edu/numimage/currency.htm.
477. The broadsides were sold for two cents a copy or one dollar for one hundred copies. Other abolitionist poems written by Whittier were "The Moral Warfare," "Massachusetts to Virginia" and "Ichabod." The latter was a scathing condemnation of Senator Daniel Webster for his support of the Fugitive Slave Act.
478. Douglass, *Narrative of the Life*, 95; Douglass, *My Bondage and My Freedom*, 359.
479. Douglass, *Narrative of the Life*, 96.
480. Douglass, *My Bondage and My Freedom*, 365.
481. Ibid., 366–67.
482. Douglass spent twenty-one months in Great Britain. In a letter he wrote to William Lloyd Garrison on January 1, 1846, he described how his life there compared with his life in the United States. The biggest difference from life in New Bedford or Boston was that in England and Ireland he never once heard the phrase "We don't allow niggers in here!"
483. Talbot County Court (Land Records) 1846–1847, MSA CE 90-63, 60 JP 35.
484. Douglass, *My Bondage and My Freedom*, 377.
485. Bordewich, *Bound for Canaan*, 114.
486. Ibid., 81.

487. New York Republican representative James Tallmadge Jr. demanded that Missouri have a plan to end slavery as a part of the government's requirement for its statehood. Berlin, *Long Emancipation*, 112.

488. Stevens, "Lone Star Diplomats," 40. The pejorative name came from the description of the American Anti-Slavery Society, which said that free speech was being "fettered and gagged" like a slave. Bordewich, *Bound for Canaan*, 155.

489. Slaves from Maryland were more successful in their escape attempts than fugitives from other slave states. *History and Statistics of the State of Maryland According to the Returns of the Seventh Census of the United States* (Washington, 1852), 35, quoted in Bridner, "Fugitive Slaves of Maryland," 33.

490. Larson, *Bound for the Promised Land*, xvi.

491. Will of Atthow Pattison, Est. #0-35-E, Dorchester County courthouse, Registrar of Wills, Cambridge, Maryland, quoted in Larson, *Bound for the Promised Land*, 5.

492. Ibid., 15.

493. Ibid., 37–38.

494. Bradford, *Harriet Tubman*, 12.

495. Bordewich, *Bound for Canaan*, 348.

496. Bradford, *Harriet Tubman*, 57. In *Bound for the Promised Land*, Larson speculates that Tubman suffered from temporal lobe epilepsy (TLE), 43.

497. For hiring practices, see Berlin, *Slaves without Masters*, 154–55.

498. Larson, *Bound for the Promised Land*, 56.

499. Ibid., 67.

500. Berlin, *Generations of Captivity*, 215. One observer of the sale of Maryland slaves to a "Georgia man" noted they "dread nothing on earth so much as this." "They regard the south with perfect horror, and to be sent there is considered as the worst punishment that could be inflicted on them." Quoted in Berlin, *Making of African America*, 106.

501. Real regional differences in bondage were reflected in the fear of slaves in the Upper South that they would be sold to the Deep South. Berlin, *Slaves without Masters*, 197.

502. Larson, *Bound for the Promised Land*, 78.

503. Ibid.

504. Bradford, *Harriet Tubman*, 17.

505. Douglass, *My Bondage and My Freedom*, 310.

506. "Harriet knew the North Star."…"That was one thing she insisted that she was always sure of." Helen Tatlock, quoted in Larson, *Bound for the Promised Land*, 80.

507. Ibid., *Bound for the Promised Land*, 80, 83.

508. Ibid., 82.

509. Ibid., 88.

510. Their sons Levin Still Jr. and Peter Still were both "sold South."

511. Bordewich, *Bound for Canaan*, 356.

512. Still, *Underground Railroad*, 161.

513. Ibid., 37.

514. Ibid., 246.

515. Ibid., 219.

516. Ibid., 213.

517. Bordewich, *Bound for Canaan*, 437. Another estimate is that between 1830 and 1860, slaves escaped at the rate of one thousand to five thousand per year. Eric Foner, *Gateway to Freedom: The Hidden History of the Underground Railroad* (New York, 2015), 4, quoted in Berlin, *Long Emancipation*, 15.

518. Berlin, *Long Emancipation*, 15–16, says the runaways were "a pervasive disturbance that infuriated the masters" and "unnerved" them. Quote from Larson, *Bound for the Promised Land*, 86.

519. Douglass, *Life and Times*, 710.

520. Brugger, *Maryland*, 257. Only nine of the fifteen slaveholding states sent delegates; most of those who attended were Tennessee locals. Sublette and Sublette, *American Slave Coast*, 573. No border states sent delegates. Bordewich, *America's Great Debate*, 257.

521. Chart statistics taken from Clark, *Eastern Shore of Maryland and Virginia*. See also Berlin, "Slave and White Populations," Tables A and B, *Slaves without Masters*, 396–99.

522. Brugger, *Maryland*, 781.

523. Whig senator James Alfred Pearce of Chestertown, Maryland, drafted the law by which Texas ceded its claims to lands in the Mexican Territory in return for the U.S. government's assumption of the state's $10 million debt. Bordewich, *America's Great Debate*, 306.

524. "Proceedings and Debates of the House of Representatives of the United States at the Second Session of the Second Congress, Began at the City of Philadelphia, November 5, 1792," Annals of Congress, 2nd Congress, 2nd Session (November 5, 1792 to March 2, 1793), 1414–15, accessed via www.ushistory.org/presidentshouse/history/slaveact1793.php.

525. See *Prigg v. Pennsylvania* 41 U.S. 539 (1842).

526. "An Act Respecting Fugitives from Justice, and Persons Escaping from the service of their Masters," in Still, *Underground Railroad*, 167–73

(quotation from 170). Berlin, in *Long Emancipation*, 79, asserts that the new act "removed the stigma of illegality and enabled kidnappers to act with impunity."

527. Wikipedia, "Ralph Waldo Emerson," last modified October 23, 2018, https://en.wikipedia.org/wiki/Ralph_Waldo_Emerson.

528. Douglass, "Internal Slave Trade," *Autobiographies*, 438, 439.

529. Larson, *Bound for the Promised Land*, 89–90.

530. Ibid., xvii, 100. Larson notes that Tubman never allowed more slaves to join her than she could look out for.

531. Ibid., xvii.

532. Ednah Dow Littlehale Chaney, "Moses," *Freedmen's Record*, March 1865, 35, quoted in Larson, *Bound for the Promised Land*, 90–91.

533. Bradford, *Harriet Tubman*, 34.

534. Ibid.

535. Larson, *Bound for the Promised Land*, 111–14, includes a vivid account of this Christmas Day escape.

536. Bradford, *Harriet Tubman*, 19.

537. The only daily newspapers were published in Baltimore, and those papers printed no Sunday editions. County papers were weekly or biweekly. Bridner, "Fugitive Slaves of Maryland," 43.

538. Ibid., 42. Weekends were also the times when slaveholders might be absent from their farms pursuing other activities.

539. Still, *Underground Railroad*, 157.

540. Bradford, *Harriet Tubman*, 14. Bradford said Tubman talked with God "as a man talketh with his friend."

541. Bordewich, *Bound for Canaan*, 350.

542. Still, *Underground Railroad*, 42–43.

543. For an informative account of Reverend Green's life, see "East New Market: Notable People and Families," www.collinsfactor.com/families/greensam.htm.

544. "Sam Green and Uncle Tom's Cabin," *Easton (MD) Gazette*, August 28, 1858, referenced in Larson, *Bound for the Promised Land*, 141.

545. Ibid., 106.

546. "Session Laws, 1841," *Archives MD* 593:232.

547. Still, *Underground Railroad*, 128–31. Reverend Green was pardoned by Governor Augustus W. Bradford in 1862 and given sixty days to leave the state.

548. Larson, *Bound for the Promised Land*, 27, 69.

549. Ibid., 143. Harriet's father had helped the "Dover Eight."

550. "Dorchester County Court Chattel Records, 1847–1852," *Archives MD* 805:163.

551. Larson, *Bound for the Promised Land*, 74, 119. Larson speculates that Rit was close to seventy.

552. Bordewich, *Bound for Canaan*, 353, suggests that Tubman's first missions were probably independent operations. By 1851, however, she had linked up with the Underground Railroad. Garrett and Still gave her money and introductions to influential abolitionists.

553. Jacobs asserted that Garrett had stolen 2,445 slaves, most of whom had come from Maryland. "Journal of the House, 1860," *Archives MD* 660:94.

554. *Baltimore American*, March 4, 1842, quoted in Berlin, *Slaves without Masters*, 210. Berlin says, "The specter of a free negro majority haunted Maryland whites."

555. Brugger, *Maryland*, 299.

556. Ibid., 268.

557. University of Virginia Library, Historical Census Browser online database, Fisher.lib.virginia.edu/collections/stats/histcensus/index.html, cited in Hait, "Identifying the Last Slave-Owner," 74.

558. Brown, *Road to Jim Crow*, 7.

559. These fears were exacerbated by the successful 1791 slave revolt in Saint-Domingue led by Toussaint L'Ouverture.

560. Quarles, in "'Freedom Fettered,'" maintains that this attitude of "fear and hostility" went back as far as the Revolutionary period when "a free black was a contradiction of the divine-right-white theory" (300) and was regarded "with more than ordinary trepidation" in the counties that depended upon tobacco (302). Berlin, *Slaves without Masters*, 354.

561. Berlin, *Slaves without Masters*, xiv, states that southern whites had learned how to deal with free blacks before the Civil War and they applied all that they had learned to limit the lives of all blacks after Emancipation. Antebellum standards of personal relations, patterns of thought and institutions remained essentially unchanged. Berlin, *Generations of Captivity*, 225, sees the regulations enacted in Delaware and Maryland during the 1840s and '50s as "precursors to postbellum black codes."

562. "Report of the Committee on Colored Population" *Maryland Legislative Documents*, 1843, doc. M, 47, quoted in Berlin, *Slaves without Masters*, 317.

563. Ibid., 95, 317, 334. Free blacks who had been convicted of a crime (even petty theft) could be auctioned off to the highest bidder for lengthy periods of what was essentially enslavement.

564. "Session Laws, 1839," *Archives MD* 600:33–34.

565. McConnell, "Black Experience in Maryland," 415.

566. Berlin, *Slaves without Masters*, 97, 233.

567. Ibid., 188. Whites also connected free blacks with rebellions (even though that was rarely the case).

568. Ibid., 369.

569. *Dred Scott v. Sandford*, 60 U.S. 393 (1857).

570. Berlin, *Slaves without Masters*, 372.

571. Brown, who had been told that Charles Sumner of Massachusetts had been attacked on the floor of the Senate, said of the Pottawatomie Creek murders, "God is my judge. We were justified under the circumstances." Bordewich, *Bound for Canaan*, 415. Brown's action followed the 1854 passage of the Kansas-Nebraska Act allowing "popular sovereignty" in those territories. After much turmoil and violence, Kansas entered the Union on January 29, 1861, as a free state.

572. John Brown to John Brown Jr., April 8, 1856, quoted in Larson, *Bound for the Promised Land*, 157–58.

573. Bordewich, *Bound for Canaan*, 418.

574. Douglass, *Life and Times*, 759.

575. Ibid., 746–47.

576. Ibid., 747.

577. The November 19, 1859 edition included a woodcut made from Martin M. Lawrence's photograph of John Brown.

578. Douglass, *Life and Times*, 761. Douglass left Canada for England on November 12, 1859. "The fact that I was now in danger of arrest on the ground of complicity with him [Brown] made what I had intended a pleasure [i.e. the trip to England] a necessity, for though in Canada, and under British law, it was not impossible that I might be kidnapped and taken to Virginia."

579. Bordewich, *America's Great Debate*, 383.

580. Brugger, *Maryland*, 272. The vote totals were: Bell 41,760 (45.14 percent), Breckinridge 42,482 (45.93 percent), Douglas 5,966 (6.45 percent) and Lincoln 2,294 (2.48 percent).

581. Jefferson Davis, *Congressional Globe* 31/1, App., 149–57, quoted in Bordewich, *America's Great Debate*, 147.

582. Alexander Stevens, March 21, 1861, quoted in https://en.wikipediaorg/wiki/Cornerstone_Speech.

583. Berlin, *Long Emancipation*, 10–11, 31, 158.

584. Goodheart, *1861*, 187, 210.

585. Mullikin, "Eastern Shore," 158. Both Eastern Shore regiments took part in the Battle of Gettysburg.

586. Larson, *Bound for the Promised Land*, 194.

587. That was about one-fifth of the black men of military age in the United States. Berlin, *Generations of Captivity*, 256.

588. "Legacy of Slavery in Maryland," *Archives MD*, http://slavery.msa.maryland.gov/html.

589. Berlin, *Generations of Captivity*, 252. Only those black soldiers who were free before April 19, 1861, received pay equity with white soldiers. Ricks, *Escape on the Pearl*, 334.

590. "Supplement to the Maryland Code, Containing the Acts of the General Assembly, Passed at the Sessions of 1861, 1861–62, 1864, 1865, 1866, and 1867," *Archives MD* 384:31. Brugger, *Maryland*, 302, says they were paid $300 by the federal government. The State of Maryland did give a $300 bonus to all who enlisted before April 1, 1864, excepting slaves. See *Archives MD* 384:30.

591. A listing of ninety-five of these Eastern Shore black soldiers from Caroline, Dorchester, Kent, Queen Anne's and Talbot Counties can be found in "Legacy of Slavery in Maryland," *Archives MD*.

592. Ricks, *Escape on the Pearl*, 334, 341. One horrible example was the massacre on April 12, 1864, at Fort Pillow, Tennessee, where over 250 Union troops—most of them African American—were slaughtered by Rebel forces.

593. "Chronology," Douglass, *Autobiographies*, 1064–65. Douglass's son Lewis fought in the Battle for Fort Wagner, South Carolina. He was not wounded, but the unit as a whole suffered severe losses.

594. Bordewich, *Bound for Canaan*, 411. Massachusetts governor John Andrew was responsible for Harriet Tubman's going to Port Royal, South Carolina. Tubman led an expedition from Port Royal twenty-five miles up the Combahee River. Larson, *Bound for the Promised Land*, 212, calls Tubman "the first woman to plan and execute an armed expedition during the Civil War."

595. Brugger, *Maryland*, 297.

596. Brown, *Road to Jim Crow*, 31.

597. Richard P. Bayly, "Proceedings of the State Convention of Maryland to Frame a New Constitution, Commenced at Annapolis, April 27, 1864," *Archives MD* 102, Volume 1, Debates: 538ff.

598. Ibid., 538–39, 542, 543. Valliant prefaced his remarks by saying that he was putting himself on record so that his descendants would know what led him to favor universal freedom.

599. Ibid., 592–604.

600. Brown, *Road to Jim Crow*, 33–34.

601. On the Eastern Shore, only the voters of Caroline County approved the Constitution (471 votes to 423). Vote totals by county can be found in the appendix to William Starr Myers, "The Maryland Constitution of 1864" (Baltimore, MD: Johns Hopkins Press, 1901) in *Archives MD* 667: 97.

602. Maryland ratified the Fourteenth Amendment on April 28, 1959. "Session Laws, 1959," *Archives MD* 642:1459. The state did not ratify the Fifteenth Amendment until May 7, 1973. "Session Laws, 1973," *Archives MD* 709:1849.

603. Douglass, "Chronology," *Autobiographies*, 1067.

604. Douglass, *Life and Times*, 877.

605. Douglass, "Chronology," *Autobiographies*, 1077.

606. Berlin, *Slaves without Masters*, 384.

Epilogue

607. In the debate over the Compromise of 1850, Senator David Yulee of Florida noted that no matter what "Yankee hypocrites" said, the North benefited from slavery just as much as the South. Bordewich, *America's Great Debate*, 41.

608. Berlin, *Many Thousands Gone*, 105. The North supplied the plantation economy capital, factorage, draft animals, food, technology and even education in the person of the plantation tutor.

609. Blackburn, *American Crucible*, 107.

610. Ibid., 305.

611. Sublette and Sublette, *American Slave Coast*, 583, quotes an Aetna advertisement from the February 21, 1860 *Statesman* (Lexington, KY).

612. "Let's Stop Fighting over History," *Baltimore Sun*, August 17, 2017, 12.

613. "Maryland." In *A Statistical Summary, State by State, of School Segregation-Desegregation in the Southern and Border Area from 1945 to the Present*, 18, https://files.eric.ed.gov/fulltext/ED019382.pdf.

REFERENCES

American Memory. "Born in Slavery: Slave Narratives from the Federal Writers' Project, 1936–1938." Library of Congress, http://memory.loc.gov/ammem/snhtml/snhome.

Ball, Charles. *Fifty Years in Chains: Or, the Life of an American Slave.* New York: H. Dayton, 1859. Available online at *North American Slave Narratives* collection of the library of the University of North Carolina at Chapel Hill, docsouth.unc.edu.

Ball, Edward. "Slavery's Trail of Tears." *Smithsonian* (November 2015): 59–82.

———. *Slaves in the Family.* New York: Farrar, Strauss & Giroux, 1998.

Baptist, Edward E. "How Slavery Haunts Today's America." CNN, September 8, 2014. CNN/2014/09/07/opinion/baptist-slavery-book-panned-economist-review/index.html.

Bast, C. Homer. "Benjamin Keene, 1694–1770: Middling Planter of Dorchester County." *Maryland Historical Magazine* 93, no. 1 (1998): 39–67.

Bell, Robert. *Book of Slave Statistics: 1864–1868, Dorchester County, Maryland.* Transcribed by Elaine McGill. N.p., n.d.

Berlin, Ira. *Generations of Captivity: A History of African-American Slaves.* Cambridge, MA: Belknap Press of Harvard University Press, 2003.

———. *The Long Emancipation: The Demise of Slavery in the United States.* Cambridge, MA: Harvard University Press, 2015.

———. *The Making of African America: The Four Great Migrations.* New York: Penguin Books, 2010.

———. *Many Thousands Gone: The First Two Centuries of Slavery in North America.* Cambridge, MA: Belknap Press of Harvard University Press, 1998.

———. *Slaves without Masters: The Free Negro in the Antebellum South.* New York: The New Press, 1974.

Blackburn, Robin. *The American Crucible: Slavery, Emancipation and Human Rights.* London: Verso, 2011.

Bordewich, Fergus M. *America's Great Debate; Henry Clay, Stephen A. Douglas, and the Compromise That Preserved the Union.* New York: Simon & Schuster, 2012.

———. *Bound for Canaan: The Epic Story of the Underground Railroad, America's First Civil Rights Movement.* New York: Amistad Press, 2006.

Bradford, Sarah. *Harriet Tubman: The Moses of Her People.* Mineola NY: Dover Publications Inc., 2004. (Originally printed by G.R. Lockwood & Son, New York, 1886. Citations refer to the 2004 edition.)

Brewington, M.V. "Shipbuilding in Maryland." In *The Old Line State: A History of Maryland*, edited by Morris L. Radoff, 238–46. Annapolis: State of Maryland Hall of Records Commission, 1971.

Bridner, Elwood L., Jr. "The Fugitive Slaves of Maryland." *Maryland Historical Magazine* 66, no. 1 (1971): 33–50.

Brown, C. Christopher. *The Road to Jim Crow: The African American Struggle on Maryland's Eastern Shore, 1860–1915.* Baltimore: Maryland Historical Society, 2016.

Browne, William Hand, Edward C. Papenfuse, et al, eds. *Archives of Maryland*, 215+ volumes. Baltimore and Annapolis, MD: 1883–. This series is ongoing and available online at http://www.msa.md.gov, where volumes, collectively or individually, can be searched electronically.

Brugger, Robert J. *Maryland: A Middle Temperament, 1634–1980.* Baltimore: Johns Hopkins University Press, in association with the Maryland Historical Society, 1988.

Calderhead, William L. "Thomas Carney: Unsung Soldier of the American Revolution." *Maryland Historical Magazine* 84, no. 4 (1989): 319–26.

Calendar of State Papers. Colonial Series 32:129. In "Maryland in 1720." *Maryland Historical Magazine* 29, no. 3 (1934): 252–55.

Carr, Lois Green. "From Servant to Freeholder: Daniel Clocker's Adventure." *Maryland Historical Magazine* 99, no. 3 (2004): 286–312.

———. "'The Metropolis of Maryland': A Comment on Town Development along the Tobacco Coast." *Maryland Historical Magazine* 69, no. 2 (1974): 124–45.

———. "Sources of Political Stability and Upheaval in Seventeenth-Century Maryland." *Maryland Historical Magazine* 79, no. 1 (1984): 44–70.

————. "St. Mary's Career Files." *Archives of Maryland*, SC 4040 and SC 5094. Available online at http://www.msa.md.gov.

Carr, Lois Green, Russell R. Menard and Lorena S. Walsh. *Robert Cole's World: Agriculture & Society in Early Maryland*. Chapel Hill: University of North Carolina Press, 1991.

Carroll, Kenneth L. "The Berry Brothers of Talbot County, Maryland: Early Antislavery Leaders." *Maryland Historical Magazine* 84, no. 1 (1989): 1–9.

————. "Maryland Quakers in the Seventeenth Century." *Maryland Historical Magazine* 42, no. 4 (1952): 297–315.

————. *Three Hundred Years and More of Third Haven Quakerism*. Easton, MD: Queen Anne Press, 1984.

————. "Voices of Protest: Eastern Shore Abolition Societies, 1790–1820." *Maryland Historical Magazine* 84, no. 4 (1989): 350–60.

Chapelle, Suzanne Ellery Greene, Jean H. Baker, Dean R. Esslinger, Whitman H. Ridgway, Jean B. Russo, Constance B. Schulz and Gregory A. Stiverson. *Maryland: A History of Its People*. Baltimore, MD: Johns Hopkins University Press, 1986.

Clark, Charles B. *The Eastern Shore of Maryland and Virginia*. Vol. 1. New York: Lewis Historical Publishing Inc., 1950.

Clayton, Ralph. "Baltimore's Own Version of 'Amistad': Slave Revolt." *Baltimore Chronicle and Sentinel*, January 7, 1998. baltimorechronicle.com/slave-ship2.html.

————. "Christmas in Baltimore for Slaves, Circa 1827." *Baltimore Chronicle and Sentinel*, December 6, 2000. baltimorechronicle.com/balto_xmas_dec00.html.

Collins, Frank. "East New Market: Notable People and Families." http://www.collinsfactor.com/families/families.htm.

Cregar, William Francis, and Dr. Christopher Johnston. "Index to Chancery Depositions, 1668–1789." *Maryland Historical Magazine* 23, no. 3 (1928): 197–242.

Crowl, Philip. "The Revolution and After: 1774–1789." In *The Old Line State: A History of Maryland*, edited by Morris L. Radoff, 35–48. Annapolis, MD: Hall of Records Commission, 1971.

Dorchester County Court, Land Records (1669–). MSA CE 46. Available online at http://www.mdlandrec.net.

Dorchester County Court (Land Records). Henry Hooper and Henry Matney to Thomas Bishop, Book HD 14, 312–13 [CR 49067, CE46-41]. Maryland State Archives.

Douglass, Frederick. *Autobiographies: Narrative of the Life of Frederick Douglass, an Ameican Slave* (1845), *My Bondage and My Freedom* (1855), *Life and Times of Frederick Douglass* (1893). Edited by Henry Louis Gates Jr. New York: Library of America, 1994.

Fausz, J. Frederick. "Present at the 'Creation': The Chesapeake World that Greeted the Maryland Colonists." *Maryland Historical Magazine* 79, no. 1 (1984): 7–20.

Fitzgerald, Frances. *The Evangelicals: The Struggle to Shape America*. New York: Simon & Schuster, 2017.

Founders Online. National Archives, http://founders.archives.gov.

Franklin, John Hope, and Alfred A. Moss Jr. *From Slavery to Freedom: A History of African Americans*. New York: McGraw-Hill, 1994.

George, Christopher T. "Mirage of Freedom: African Americans in the War of 1812." *Maryland Historical Magazine* 107, no. 1 (2012): 37–55.

Goldsborough, Charles. "Governor Charles Goldsborough's Views on Slavery." *Maryland Historical Magazine* 39, no. 4 (1944): 332–34. (Letter to Dr. Vans M. Sulivane on August 28, 1834.)

Goodheart, Adam. *1861: The Civil War Awakening*. New York: Alfred A. Knopf, 2011.

Hait, Michael. "Identifying the Last Slave-Owner of Freedmen in Maryland Using Local Records." *Maryland Genealogical Society Journal* 51, no. 1 (2010): 73–88.

Hall, Clayton Colman, ed. *Narratives of Early Maryland History, 1633–1684*. New York: Charles Scribner's Sons, 1910.

Hedberg, Jacqueline H. "The Bishops of Hoopers Island—Slave and Free." *Maryland Genealogical Society Journal* 51, no. 1 (2010): 89–110.

Heinegg, Paul. *Free African Americans of Maryland and Delaware: From the Colonial Period to 1810*. Baltimore, MD: Clearfield, 2000.

Henry, Jane. "The Choptank Indians of Maryland under the Proprietary Government." *Maryland Historical Magazine* 65, no. 2 (1970): 171–80.

Jacobs, Harriet A. *Incidents in the Life of a Slave Girl*. Boston: Published for the author, 1861, edited by L. Marie Francis. Available online at North American Slave Narratives collection of the library of the University of North Carolina at Chapel Hill, docsouth.unc.edu.

Jeske, Mary Clement. "From Slave to Slave Owner: The Life of Robert Pearle of Maryland." *Maryland Historical Magazine* 103, no. 1 (2008): 4–31.

Johnson, Whittington B. "The Origin and Nature of African Slavery in Seventeenth Century Maryland." *Maryland Historical Magazine* 73, no. 3 (1978): 236–45.

Jones, Elias. *New Revised History of Dorchester County, Maryland.* Cambridge, MD: Tidewater Publishers, 1902. Revised in 1925. Added to and corrected by daughter Mary Ruth Jones in 1966. (Citations refer to the 1966 edition.)

Karinen, Arthur E. "Maryland Population 1634–1730: Numerical and Distributional Aspects." *Maryland Historical Magazine* 54, no. 4 (1959): 365–407.

Kimmel, Ross M. "Free Blacks in Seventeenth Century Maryland." *Maryland Historical Magazine* 71, no. 1 (1976): 19–25.

Land, Aubrey C. "The Colonial Period." In *The Old Line State: A History of Maryland*, edited by Morris L. Radoff, 11–34. Annapolis, MD: Hall of Records Commission, 1971.

———. "The Planters of Colonial Maryland." *Maryland Historical Magazine* 67, no. 2 (1972): 109–28.

"Land Notes 1634–1655." *Maryland Historical Magazine* 9, no. 3 (1914): 290–96.

Larson, Kate Clifford. *Bound for the Promised Land: Harriet Tubman, Portrait of an American Hero.* New York: Ballantine Books, 2004.

"Maryland." In *A Statistical Summary, State by State, of School Segregation-Desegregation in the Southern and Border Area from 1945 to the Present*, 18. Nashville, TN: Southern Education Reporting Service, 1967. Accessed October 30, 2018. https://files.eric.ed.gov/fulltext/ED019382.pdf.

Maryland State Archives. "Legacy of Slavery in Maryland." http://slavery.msa.maryland.gov.

McConnell, Roland C. "The Black Experience in Maryland: 1634–1900." In *The Old Line State: A History of Maryland*, edited by Morris L. Radoff, 405–32. Annapolis: Hall of Records Commission State of Maryland, Publication No. 16, 1971.

Menard, Russell R. "Population, Economy, and Society in Seventeenth-Century Maryland." *Maryland Historical Magazine* 79, no. 1 (1984): 71–92.

Middleton, Arthur Pierce. *Tobacco Coast: A Maritime History of Chesapeake Bay in the Colonial Era.* Baltimore: Johns Hopkins University Press and the Maryland State Archives, 1984.

Middleton, Arthur Pierce, and Henry M. Miller. "'Mr. Secretary': John Lewgar, St. John's Freehold, and Early Maryland." *Maryland Historical Magazine* 103, no 2. (2008): 132–65.

Miller, M. Sammy. "Patty Cannon: Murderer and Kidnapper of Free Blacks: A Review of the Evidence." *Maryland Historical Magazine* 72, no. 3 (1977): 419–23.

Morgan, Edmund S. *American Slavery, American Freedom: The Ordeal of Colonial Virginia.* New York: W.W. Norton & Company, 1975.

Morgan, Michael. *Delmarva's Patty Cannon: The Devil on the Nanticoke.* Charleston, SC: The History Press, 2015.

Morison, Samuel Eliot, and Henry Steele Commager. *The Growth of the American Republic.* Vol. 1, 4th ed. New York: Oxford University Press, 1956.

Mowbray, Calvin W., and Mary I. Mowbray. *The Early Settlers of Dorchester County and Their Lands.* Westminster, MD: Willow Bend Books, 1992.

Mullikin, James C. "The Eastern Shore." In *The Old Line State: A History of Maryland*, edited by Morris L. Radoff, 149–61. Annapolis: Hall of Records Commission State of Maryland, Publication No. 16, 1971.

Neill, Edward D. *Terra Mariae: Threads of Maryland Colonial History.* Philadelphia: J.B. Lippincott & Company, 1867.

Neimeyer, Charles Patrick. *War in the Chesapeake: The British Campaigns to Control the Bay, 1813–1814.* Annapolis, MD: Naval Institute Press, 2015.

Nix, Amanda, and Travis Hess. "Preserving the Warden House—And Baltimore's Slavery Past." *Baltimore Sun,* June 16, 2016, 17.

Nye, Eric W. "Pounds Sterling to Dollars: Historical Conversion of Currency." University of Wyoming. Accessed October 30, 2018. http://www.uwyo.edu/numimage/currency.htm.

Porter, Frank W., III. "A Century of Accommodation: The Nanticoke Indians in Colonial Maryland." *Maryland Historical Magazine* 74, no. 2 (1979): 175–92.

"Prerogative Court (Inventories and Accounts)." Huntington Collection of Maryland State Archives Security Microfilm 1945–1946. Archives of Maryland. TE1, http://guide.mdsa.net.

"Prerogative Court (Wills) 1635–1777." Archives of Maryland. S538, http://guide.mdsa.net.

Quarles, Benjamin. "'Freedom Fettered': Blacks in the Constitutional Era in Maryland, 1776–1810." *Maryland Historical Magazine* 84, no. 4 (1989): 299–304.

Radoff, Morris L. "The Settlement." In *The Old Line State: A History of Maryland*, edited by Morris L. Radoff, 1–10. Annapolis: Hall of Records Commission State of Maryland, Publication No. 16, 1971.

Reséndez, Andrés. *The Other Slavery: The Uncovered Story of Indian Enslavement in America.* New York: Houghton Mifflin Harcourt, 2016.

Ricks, Mary Kay. *Escape on the Pearl: The Heroic Bid for Freedom on the Underground Railroad.* New York: HarperCollins, 2007.

Robinson, W. Stitt. "Conflicting Views on Landholding: Lord Baltimore and the Experiences of Colonial Maryland with Native Americans." *Maryland Historical Magazine* 83, no. 2 (1988): 85–97.

Rountree, Helen C., and Thomas E. Davidson. *Eastern Shore Indians of Virginia and Maryland.* Charlottesville: University Press of Virginia, 1997.

Scharf, J. Thomas. *History of Maryland: From the Earliest Period to the Present Day.* Vol. 1, *1600–1765.* Hatboro, PA: Tradition Press, 1967.

Schermerhorn, Calvin. "What Else You Should Know about Baltimore." Columbian College of Arts & Sciences. historynewsnetwork.org/article/159294.

Shane, Scott. "The Secret History of City Slave Trade." *Baltimore Sun*, June 20, 1999.

Skordas, Gust. *The Early Settlers of Maryland.* Baltimore, MD: Genealogical Publishing Company, 1968.

Small, Clara L. "Abolitionists, Free Blacks, and Runaway Slaves: Surviving Slavery on Maryland's Eastern Shore." University of Delaware, last modified August 4, 1997. www1.udel.edu/BlackHistory/abolitionists.html.

Smith, Robyn N. "Minty's Legacy: A Black Family in Slavery and Freedom." *Maryland Genealogical Society Journal* 67, no. 1 (2016): 7–36.

Stein, Charles Francis. *A History of Calvert County Maryland.* Self-published in cooperation with the Calvert County Historical Society, 1960.

Stevens, Kenneth R. "Lone Star Diplomats: Representatives of the Republic of Texas in Washington." *Capitol Dome* 54, no. 1 (2017): 36–48.

Stevenson, Brenda E. *What Is Slavery?* Malden, MA: Polity Press, 2015.

Still, William. *The Underground Railroad: Authentic Narratives and First-Hand Accounts.* Mineola, NY: Dover Publications, 2007. (Originally published in 1872. Citations refer to the 2007 edition.)

Sublette, Ned, and Constance Sublette. *The American Slave Coast: A History of the Slave-Breeding Industry.* Chicago: Lawrence Hill Books, 2016.

Sullivan, Patricia. "Healing a Painful Past." *Washington Post*, February 11, 2018, C1 and C6.

Swarns, Rachel L. "272 Slaves Were Sold to Save Georgetown. What Does It Owe Their Descendants?" *New York Times.* April 17, 2016. http://www.nytimes.com/2016/04/17/us/georgetown-university-search-for-slave-descendants.html.

Talbot County Court, Land Records (1669–). MSA CE 92. Available online at http://www.mdlandrec.net.

Thomas, Hugh. *The Slave Trade: The Story of the Atlantic Slave Trade 1440–1870.* New York: Simon & Schuster Paperbacks, 1997.

Thomas, James W. *Chronicles of Colonial Maryland.* Cumberland, MD: Eddy Press Corporation, 1913.

Torrence, Clayton. *Old Somerset on the Eastern Shore of Maryland: A Study in Foundations and Founders.* Baltimore, MD: Regional Publishing Company, 1979.

Townsend, George Alfred "Gath." *The Entailed Hat, or Patty Cannon's Times: A Romance.* Cambridge, MD: Tidewater Publishers, 1955. (Originally published in 1884. Citations refer to the 1955 edition.)

Tyler, John W. "Foster Cunliffe and Sons: Liverpool Merchants in the Maryland Tobacco Trade, 1738–1765." *Maryland Historical Magazine* 73, no. 3 (1978): 246–79.

Walsh, Lorena S. "Rural African Americans in the Constitutional Era in Maryland, 1776–1810." *Maryland Historical Magazine* 84, no. 4 (1989): 327–41.

Wax, Darold D. "Black Immigrants: The Slave Trade in Colonial Maryland." *Maryland Historical Magazine* 73, no. 1 (1978): 30–45.

Wright, James M. *The Free Negro in Maryland: 1634–1860.* New York: Octagon Books, 1971. Originally published by the Columbia University Press, 1921. (Citations refer to the 1971 edition.)

Wright, Louis B. *The Cultural Life of the American Colonies.* Mineola, NY: Dover Publications, 2002. (Originally published by Harper & Row, 1957. Citations refer to the 2002 edition.)

INDEX

ABOUT THE AUTHOR

Jacqueline Simmons Hedberg was born in Dorchester County on Hoopers Island, where her family has lived since the island's first settlement over 350 years ago.

Since her retirement from a long career teaching history in the Baltimore County Public Schools in Maryland and for the Department of Defense Overseas Schools in Germany and Japan, she has devoted her time to researching family genealogy and the history of Hoopers Island.

She is the author of several books about her birthplace, including *Hoopers Island* and *Hoopers Island's Changing Face* (Arcadia Publishing's Images of America series). In 2010, she received the Maryland Historical Society's Marion Brewington Prize for her essay "Humes Wallace, Hoopers Island Boat Builder." She has also written frequently about her family history for the *Maryland Genealogical Society Journal*.

In 2000, she and her husband organized the Friends of the Old Hoopers Island Graveyard to save an "Endangered Maryland Treasure," and in 2010, they published an illustrated inventory of the largest cemetery on the island—*We Once Lived on Hoopers Island: Remembering Those Buried in Hosier Memorial Cemetery*.

The author lives in Baltimore, Maryland.